BAD ELSTER

Landschaft und Geschichte

Sachsenbuch

Die Farbtafeln stellten uns zur Verfügung:
Colorfoto Schlegel, Lunzenau: S. 38 und Einbandmotive
Engel Luftbild, Coburg: S. 46/47
Kilu minh Viet: S. 63
Werner Neumeister, München: S. 47
alle anderen: Karlheinz Blei und Joachim Dick, Erlbach

Einbandmotive:
Kurhaus, 1888 bis 1890 durch Landbaumeister Trobsch,
Zwickau, errichtet (vorn).
Elsterbrunnen vor der Wandelhalle (hinten).

Cover photos:
Spa house built in 1888–90 by master builder Trobsch,
Zwickau. (front)
Elster fountain in front of the pump house. (back)

Lektorat und Bildbeschaffung: Wolfgang Tittel
Übersetzung: Gabriele Graf und Herbert R. Nestler

Folgende Autoren haben unter Leitung von Christoph Flämig
den Text verfaßt:
Martin Schwarzenberg (Geschichte)
Horst Wunderlich (Stadtgestaltung/Architektur)
Gerhard Brunner (Kurgeschichte)
Heinrich Wagner (Umgebung)

Sonderausgabe
Sachsenbuch Verlagsgesellschaft mbH, Leipzig
© 1992 by I. P. Verlagsgesellschaft
International Publishing GmbH, München
Reproarbeiten: Fotolito Longo, Frangart
Satz: Satz & Repro Grieb, München
Gesamtherstellung: Brepols SA, Turnhout, Belgien

ISBN 3-910148-44-1

Perle des Vogtlandes

Seinen Namen hat «das Land an der oberen Weißen Elster um Plauen, Weida und Gera» von den kaiserlichen Vögten, die eben dort ihren Sitz hatten. Neben den sächsischen und thüringischen Landesteilen nehmen auch die Gegend um Hof – als «Bayerisches Vogtland» – und die Gebiete um Cheb (Eger) und Aš (Asch) die Bezeichnung Vogtland für sich in Anspruch, da sie ebenfalls zeitweilig unter Herrschaft der Vögte standen. Schon im 14. Jahrhundert verloren diese größere Gebietsteile vor allem an die Wettiner. 1547 gelang es einem von ihnen, das ganze historische Vogtland wieder an sich zu bringen, das jedoch 1569 von Kursachsen durch Kauf erworben wurde.

Deutschstämmige Siedler aus Thüringen, Franken und Bayern kamen ab dem 12. Jahrhundert in dieses Gebiet. Die Gegend um Klingenthal und Markneukirchen wurde in ihrer Entwicklung stark durch die im 17. Jahrhundert einwandernden böhmischen Exulanten geprägt. Sie brachten die Herstellung von Musikinstrumenten in den Raum, wodurch dieser Landstrich eine bedeutende Exportindustrie erhielt. Aus den großen Wäldern im gebirgigen Teil wurden reiche Holzvorräte einer gewerblichen Nutzung zugeführt und auf den Flüssen in das holzarme Niederland geflößt.

«The land along the upper Weisse Elster River around Plauen, Weida and Gera» gets its name from the imperial landvogts who had their seat there. Apart from the Saxonian and Thuringian parts of the country, also the area around Hof – as «Bavarian Vogtland» – and the areas around (Cheb) Eger and (As) Asch lay claim to the term vogtland since they as well were temporarily under the rule of the landvogts. Already in the 14th century they lost major parts of the region, primarily to the Wettin dynasty. In 1547 one of them succeeded in bringing the entire historical Vogtland under his rule again, but it was purchased in 1569 by the electorate of Saxony.

Settlers of German origin from Thuringia, Franconia and Bavaria came into this area starting in the 12th century. The region around Klingenthal and Markneukirchen was strongly influenced in its development by the Bohemian exiles who immigrated in the 17th century. They brought the manufacturing of musical instruments to the area and thus gave this region an important export industry. From the large forests in the mountainous section rich timber was provided for commercial use and rafted on the rivers to the plain which was deficient in wood.

In Plauen als der Hauptstadt des Vogtlandes entfaltete sich die Tuchmacherei, die sich seit dem frühen 17. Jahrhundert auf die Herstellung feiner Baumwollgewebe («Plauener Spitze») umstellte. Eine Besonderheit in dieser Gegend war die Perlenfischerei in der Elster. Möglich, daß die Bezeichnung «Perle des Vogtlandes» für Bad Elster auch damit in Zusammenhang steht, wahrscheinlich aber ist sie eher auf die Erscheinung und natürliche Lage der Stadt zurückzuführen.

Das Heilbad Bad Elster liegt im Dreiländereck zwischen Böhmen, Bayern und Sachsen.

Eine reizvolle Mittelgebirgslandschaft steigt hier nach Süden hin an bis zu ihrem höchsten Berg, dem 759 Meter hohen Kapellenberg. Nach der im Kammgebiet in der CSFR entspringenden Weißen Elster trägt der Gebirgszug den Namen Elstergebirge. Als südlicher und zugleich höchster Teil des Vogtlandes wird das Gebiet auch als Oberes Vogtland bezeichnet.

Bad Elster liegt geschützt (450–500 m) im Tal der Weißen Elster, rings umgeben von dichtbewaldeten Bergen. Die kleine Stadt (3800 Einwohner) scheint direkt mit ihrer Umgebung verwachsen. Hier, in der unteren Region des Elstergebirges, wirkt ein subalpines Klima als Erholungs- und Heilfaktor, das besonders für Herz- und Kreislaufkranke wertvoll ist. Die mittlere jährliche Lufttemperatur beträgt ca. 7 Grad und liegt damit um 3 Grad niedriger als im Flachland. Mit zunehmender Höhenlage verzögert sich dadurch die Entwicklung der Vegetation und so kann mancher Besucher den Frühling ein zweites Mal erleben, wenn er die gleiche Blühphase hier noch einmal beobachtet, die vor seiner Abreise im Unterland bereits abgeschlossen war. Besonders angenehm wird die etwas niedrigere Temperatur während der Sommermonate empfunden. In dieser Zeit der Hochsaison findet man in der waldreichen Umgebung einen erfrischenden Aufenthalt. Die günstigen Luftverhältnisse haben zusammen mit der Heilwirkung der verschiedenen Quellen Bad Elster als einen der ältesten Kurorte Deutschlands und seit 1848 als «Königliches Staatsbad» berühmt gemacht.

In Plauen, capital of the Vogtland, clothmaking developed which since the early 17th century turned to the production of fine cotton cloth («Plauen lace»). A specialty in this area was pearl fishing in the Elster River. It is possible that the term «pearl of the Vogtland» for Bad Elster is also connected with this fact, but it is more likely that it is due to the appearance and the natural location of the town.

The health resort of Bad Elster is located in the tri-country intersection of Bohemia, Bavaria and Saxony.

A charming low mountain range ascends here to the south up to its ultimate peak, the 759 meter (2,490 foot) Kapellenberg. The mountain range acquired its name, Elstergebirge, from the Weisse Elster River which originates on its crest. As the southernmost and at the same time highest part of the Vogtland, the area is also called Upper Vogtland.

Bad Elster lies protected (altitude of 450 – 500 meters [1,475–1,640 feet]) in the valley of the Weisse Elster River surrounded by densely wooded mountains. The small town (3,800 inhabitants) seems to have grown into its surroundings. Here in the lower region of the Elster Mountains a subalpine climate provides a factor of recreation and healing which is especially valuable for people suffering from coronary or circulatory diseases. The average annual air temperature is approximately 7 degrees C (45 degrees F) and is thus 3 degrees C (5 degrees F) lower than in the plain. With increasing elevation the development of the vegetation is delayed and thus many a visitor can experience spring a second time when again observing the same blooming phase which was already completed before his departure from the lowlands. The somewhat moderated temperature is felt to be agreeable during the summer months. In this time of the high season the surroundings rich in wood make for a refreshing stay. The favorable condition of the air together with the healing effects of the various springs have made Bad Elster famous as one of the oldest health resorts in Germany and since 1848 as «royal state bath».

Das Kurzentrum 1903, aufgenommen und gezeichnet von G. Walter, Freiberg i. Sa., Koloriertes Original 3160 × 1570 mm.

The spa center in 1903 taken and drawn by G. Walter, Freiberg i.Sa., colored original 3.160 by 1.570 mm (12.44 by 6.18 inches).

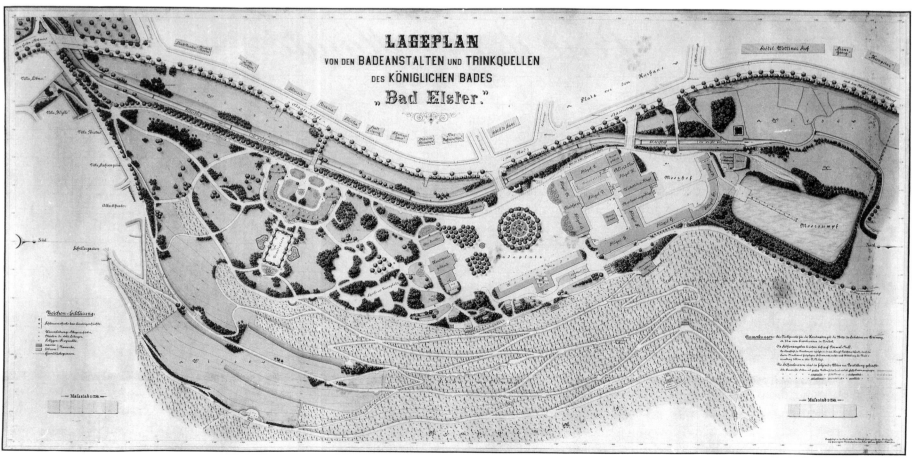

Bad Elster im Wandel der Jahrhunderte

Die Anfänge der Besiedlungsgeschichte des obervogtländischen Raumes lassen sich weit zurückverfolgen. Interessant sind Knochenfunde aus der Steinzeit, genauer aus dem Pleistozän (Eiszeit), also etwa 600 000 bis 12 000 Jahre v. Chr. Sie wurden nahe der Kreisstadt, in Untermarxgrün, entdeckt. Es handelt sich um Reste von Nashorn, Wildpferd und Mammut, deren Beschaffenheit ein willkürliches Zerschlagen schlußfolgern läßt. Das weist auf Aktivitäten eiszeitlicher Jäger hin. Weitere Funde, insbesondere Siedlungsfunde fehlen. So kann das Gebiet in dieser Zeit nur Durchzugsgebiet, z. B. aus dem fruchtbaren Thüringer Saaletal in das Böhmische Egertal, gewesen sein.

Andere Funde aus diesem Raum fallen in die Mittel- und Jungsteinzeit. Rest von Feuersteinwerkzeugen wurden u. a. in Taltitz, Untertriebel, Raun und Hohendorf gefunden. Aber auch hier kann man nur von beim Durchzug «verlorengegangenen» Werkzeugen, nicht aber von Siedlungsbeweisen sprechen.

Der nächste Mosaikstein der Frühgeschichte ist ein Armring, der in Oelsnitz gefunden wurde. Er stammt aus der Bronzezeit (1800 bis 800 Jahre v. Chr.).

Erst Keramikfunde von Taltitz-Dobeneck beweisen, daß Menschen in dem Gebiet gesiedelt haben. Sie wurden von Amandus Haase beim Talsperren- und Autobahnbau ausgegraben. Zeitlich sind sie in die jüngere Bronzezeit einzuordnen.

Der Schlackenwall am Eisenberg bei Pöhl wird als Rest einer frühzeitlichen Volksburg angesehen, Scherbenfunde lassen vermuten, daß sie möglicherweise ständig bewohnt war. Danach gehört die Siedlung schon in den Beginn der Eisenzeit (800 bis 500 Jahre v. Chr.).

Aus der Zeitspanne von 400 v. Chr. bis 600 n. Chr. fehlen jegliche Hinweise auf die Existenz von Menschen.

Der nächste Fund im Lauf der Frühgeschichte stammt aus der Slawenzeit. Es ist eine Scherbe, die beim Bau des Elsterbades in Oelsnitz gefunden wurde. Sie datiert aus der mittelslawischen Periode (800 bis 1000 n. Chr.). Trotz dieses Fundes sind Anfang und Ende der slawischen Besiedelung des Raumes weitgehend unklar. Ortsnamen, die auf «itz» enden, weisen daraufhin. So ist eine dünne Besiedelung im Bereich der Kreisstadt, also nördlich von Adorf und Bad Elster, in der slawischen Periode zu vermuten.

Dagegen ist anzunehmen, daß das Ortsgebiet im gesamten beschriebenen Zeitraum unbesiedelt war. Die Höhen waren von undurchdringlichem Ur-Mischwald (Miriquidi-Wald) besetzt und die Täler durch Sumpf- und Überschwemmungsgebiete der Weißen Elster und ihrer zufließenden Bäche schwer passierbar.

Nach der Jahrtausendwende setzt die deutsche Besiedelung und Christianisierung dieses Gebietes ein. Die ersten Beweise dafür liefern Urkunden. So soll der Name des Flusses «Elster» in Form von «Elstrit», «Elstret», «Elstrat» schon im 10. Jahrhundert erscheinen. Sicher ist die Erwähnung des Flusses als Grenze des Pfarrsprengels in der Gründungsurkunde der Plauener Johanniskirche von 1122.

Eine wesentliche Rolle bei der Christianisierung und Besiedelung des Vogtlandes spielte der Deutsche Ritterorden. Die Mönche leisteten Pionierarbeit bei der Führung der Siedler und Urbarmachung des Landes. Interessant ist, daß dies aus zwei Richtungen geschah. So hatte der Deutsche Ritterorden um 1289 ein Deutsches Haus in Adorf von Asch aus gegründet. Asch gehörte zum Bistum Regensburg und zum Erzbistum Salzburg. Dagegen war bei der Gründung der Plauener Johanniskirche 1122 der Naumburger Bischof Dietrich federführend. Das Bistum Naumburg gehörte zum Erzbistum Magdeburg.

Ein weiterer Beleg für die beiden Richtungen ist die Mundartgrenze. So kamen aus dem Westen oberfränkische Siedler und kultivierten das Land nördlich dieser Grenze. Aus dem Süden kamen die Ober-

Bad Elster in the Change of the Centuries

The beginnings of the settlement history of the Upper Vogtland can be traced far back. Interesting are bone findings from the Stone Age, to be more specific from the Pleistocene (Ice Age) approximately 600,000 to 12,000 B. C. They were discovered close to the district town of Untermarxgruen. They were the remains of rhinoceros, wild horse and mammoth, the nature of which leads one to the assumption that they were deliberately crushed. This suggests the activity of hunters from the Ice Age. There are no further findings, especially of settlements. Thus the area at that time can only have been a region of transit, for example from the fertile valley of the Thuringian Saale River to the Bohemian valley of the Eger River.

Other findings from this area date back to the Mesolithic and Neolithic periods. Remains of firestone tools were found in Taltitz, Untertriebel, Raun and Hohendorf and elsewhere. But also in this case one can only speak of tools «lost» in transit, but not evidence of settlement.

The next mosaic piece of early history is an armband which was found in Oelsnitz. It dates back to the Bronze Age (1,800–800 B.C.).

First ceramic findings of Taltitz-Dobeneck prove that people settled in this area. They were excavated by Amandus Haase during construction of dams and highways. From a chronological point of view, they belong to the Younger Bronze Age.

The slag rampart at Eisenberg Mountain at Poehl is regarded as a leftover from a prehistoric people's fortress, findings of broken pieces lead to the assumption that it may have been permanently inhabited. According to this, the settlement already existed at the beginning of the Iron Age (800–500 B.C.).

From the period between 400 B.C. and A.D. 600 there are no hints whatsoever about the presence of humans.

The next finding in the course of early history stems from the Slavic period. It is a broken artifact which was found during the construction of the Elster Bath in Oelsnitz. It dates back to the Middle Slavic Period (A.D. 800–1000). Despite this discovery, the beginning and end of the Slavic settlement in this region are largely unclear. Village names ending in «itz» allude to this fact. Therefore a sparse population in the region of the district town, that is to say to the north of Adorf and Bad Elster, is assumed to have existed in the Slavic period.

One however assumes that the village area was not settled throughout the described period of time. The elevations were covered with an impenetrable jungle of mixed forest (Miriquidi Forest) and the valleys were hard to pass due to the swamps and inundated zones of the Weisse Elster River and its tributaries.

After the turn of the millennium the German settlement and Christianization of this area began. The first evidence is provided by documents. It is said that the name of the river «Elster» appears in the form of «Elstrit», «Elstret», and «Elstrat» already in the 10th century. The mention of the river as border of the parish is confirmed in the founding document of the Plauen Johannes Church in 1122.

The Teutonic Order played an important role in the Christianization and settlement of the Vogtland. The monks did pioneer work in the guidance of the settlers and reclamation of the country. It is interesting that this was done from two directions. Thus the Teutonic Order had founded a German House in Adorf of Asch in 1289. Asch belonged to the Bishopric of Regensburg and the Archbishopric of Salzburg. In the foundation of the Plauen Johannes Church in 1122 on the other hand the Naumburg Bishop Dietrich was instrumental. The Bishopric of Naumburg belonged to the Archbishopric of Magdeburg.

Further evidence for these two directions is the border of dialects. From the west Upper Franconian settlers came and cultivated the

pfälzer und machten das Territorium der heutigen Stadt urbar. Dabei hat offensichtlich das schon bestehende Kloster Waldsassen als Basis für den Deutschen Ritterorden eine wesentliche Rolle gespielt.

Möglicherweise entstand schon um 1100 die frühdeutsche Ringwallanlage – das «alte Schloß» im Zeidelweidetal zur Sicherung der Kolonisation. Wahrscheinlich handelte es sich hierbei nur um ein Gebäude (Wachturm) mit Pallisade und Wassergraben. Bereits 1455 lag die Wasserburg wüst, aber noch heute sind Ringwallinsel und Wassergraben als Bodendenkmal zu besichtigen.

Die Egerländer Herrschaft Asch trieb von Burg Neuberg aus (heute Podhradi, CSFR) Tochterherrschaften in die Grenzwälder des Elstergebirges. Außer Selb entstand auch Adorf in dieser Zeit.

Die älteste nachweisbare Erwähnung des Ortes «Elster» findet man in einer Urkunde aus dem Jahre 1324. Hier erscheint Elster als «Sitz des Ritters Conrad, einer der Herren von Neiperg, die zwischen Elster und Asch ihre Neiperger Namensburg hatten.» Am 3. Oktober 1324 gelobten Conrad und seine Söhne Konrad und Eberhard «auf ihrem Hofe keinen Feind der Egerer zu behausen und keinen Schaden von da aus zu tun.» Das Original dieser Urkunde befindet sich im Stadtarchiv von Cheb (Eger).

Nach Dr. Flechsig, dem ersten Elsteraner Bade- und Brunnenarzt, steht außer Zweifel, daß der «Gesundbrunnen von Elster» schon im Mittelalter bekannt war. So hätten die alten Wahlen oder Venetianer, welche im 13./14. Jahrhundert das Vogtland durchstreiften, um Gold, Edelsteine und Flußperlen zu suchen, die Quelle hoch geschätzt. Das «Wahlenbüchlein» sagt, daß sie «zur Leibesnotdurft gar wohl dienlich und absonderlich gegen die bösen Leibeswetter zu gebrauchen sei.»

Wie schon erwähnt, waren 1324 die Herren von Neuberg die politischen Herren von Elster. Daß sie in Elster ihren Sitz hatten, geht aus der Formulierung in den alten Urkunden hervor. So muß man schon in dieser Zeit von der Existenz eines Rittergutes und damit auch eines Dorfes, dessen Bewohner die Führung eines solchen feudalen Hofes gewährleisten konnten, ausgehen. Die Herren von Neuberg werden außer 1324 noch in Urkunden vom 13.12.1335 und aus

land to the north of this border. From the south the people from Upper Palatine came and reclaimed the territory of today's town. In this the already existing Waldsassen monastery obviously played an important role as basis for the Teutonic Order.

It is possible that the early German rampart facility – the «Old Castle» in the valley of the Zeitelweide for the purpose of securing colonization – already developed around 1100. It is likely that it consisted of only one building (watchtower) with palisade and moat. Already in 1455 the water fortress was deserted but the rampart island and the moat can still today be visited as monuments.

The Egerland's Asch rulers from their Fort Neuberg Castle (today Podhradi, Czechoslovakia) established affiliate territories in the border forests of the Elster Mountains. Selb as well as Adorf developed in this period.

The oldest provable mention of the village «Elster» can be found in a document from 1322. Here Elster appears as «seat of Knight Conrad, one of the masters of Neiperg, who had their Neiperg Castle between Elster and Asch». On October 3, 1324 Conrad and his sons Konrad and Eberhard promised «not to accommodate in their court any enemy of the Egers and not to do any damage from there». The original of this document can now be found in the city archives of Eger (today Cheb, Czechoslovakia).

According to Dr. Flechsig, the first bath and spring doctor from Elster, there is no doubt that the «healing spring of Elster» was already known in the Middle Ages. He maintains that the old Wahlen or Venetians, who in the 13th and 14th centuries traversed the Vogtland in order to search for gold, precious stones and river pearls, highly appreciated the spring. The «booklet of the Wahlen» says that it was «very beneficial for bodily necessities and strangely helpful against bad physical ailments».

As already mentioned, the masters of Neuberg were the political rulers of Elster in 1324. The fact that they had their seat in Elster is obvious from phrases used in old documents. Therefore it must be assumed that already at that time a knight's estate existed and thus also a village whose inhabitants guaranteed the presence of such a

Das Rittergut Elster um 1855.
The Knight's Estate of Elster around 1855.

den Jahren 1374 und 1380 namentlich als Besitzer von Elster erwähnt. 1413 erhält der «ehrbare und feste Heinrich von Czedewitz (Zedt-witz) die «Anteile an der Herrschaft Asch», die ein «Chunrat von Neuberg, zu Elster gesessen, und seine Söhne» ihm verkaufen. Mit dieser Formulierung wird der Besitzwechsel des Rittergutes Elster beschrieben.

Zwei weitere Urkunden aus dem 15. Jahrhundert zeugen von Elster: 1439 werden der «Wirtin Gertruden 400 Rh.fl. am Sattelhofe zu Elster zum Leibgedinge geliehen». Am interessantesten ist eine Urkunde von 1414. Es ist ein Lehensbrief über «10 Höfe und 6 Her-bergen zu Elster». Hier werden die Höfe und Herbergen genauer bezeichnet: «der Uebels, der Heidenreichs, Hans Müllers, Peters, Ha-fersentens und Peter Herbigs Höfe, der Hof bei dem Borne (Quel-le/Brunnen!) und der auf dem Steine, sowie die Herbergen des Mader, Kolmar, Möchen (Mönnich?), Keysitz, der Osterheldin und der Rot-koppin». Damit haben wir ein fast 600 Jahre altes, erstes Einwohner-verzeichnis von Elster! Das alte Dorfgebiet lag um das Rittergut im Gelände des heutigen Rosengartens und im Kesselbachtal aufwärts. Die Bewohner waren arme zins- und frondienstpflichtige Bauern. Ob sie 1430 von den sich nach Böhmen zurückziehenden Hussiten, die vorher Oelsnitz und Plauen gebrandschatzt hatten, überfallen wur-den, ist nicht belegt. Ebenso ist die Beteiligung der Elsteraner Bauern am Bauernkrieg nicht exakt nachzuweisen. Wahrscheinlich haben sich aber auch Elsteraner Ende April 1525 «mit der Bauernschaft des südlichen Landgerichts Adorf bei Landwüst im Feldlager» getroffen. Jedenfalls hielt Kurfürst Johann von Sachsen persönlich vom 30. Juni bis 1. Juli des gleichen Jahres in Plauen Gericht über die «Aufrührer». Dabei wurden über sämtliche Dörfer des Amtes Vogtsberg, also wohl ebenfalls über Elster, Geldstrafen verhängt.

Sehr wahrscheinlich stand zu dieser Zeit schon die alte Elsteraner Dorfkirche. In der Überlieferung wird sogar von einer «Frühmeß- und Wallfahrtskirche» gesprochen. Allein auf dem Kirchberg ste-hend, könnte sie schon vor der Siedelung der ersten Elsteraner Bauern bestanden haben. Mit Sicherheit sind an dem 1892 abgebrochenen alten Sakralbau aber romanische Elemente sichtbar gewesen. So han-delte es sich bei den kleinen Fenstern im unteren Teil des Turmes um

feudal court. The masters of Neuberg are mentioned by name, apart from 1324 also in documents dated December 13, 1335 as well as 1374 and 1380, as the owners of Elster.

In 1413 the «honorable and firm Heinrich von Czedewitz» (Zedt-witz) received the «shares in the Asch rule» which were sold to him by a «Chunrat of Neuberg seated at Elster and his sons». This is how the change of ownership of the knight's estate Elster is phrased.

Two other documents from the 15th century testify to Elster: in 1439 the «innkeeper Gertruden» was lent «400 Rh.fl. at the Sattelhof court at Elster for retirement». The most interesting is a document dated 1414. It is an enfeoffment for «10 courts and 6 inns at Elster». Here the courts and inns are described more specifically: «of the Uebels, the Heidenreichs, of Hans Mueller, of the Peters, Hafersen-tens, and Peter Herbig's courts, the court at the spring and the one at the stone as well as the inns of Mader, Kolmar, Moechen (Moen-nich?), Keysitz, of the Osterheldin and the Rotkoppin». Thus we have an almost 600 year-old first record of inhabitants of Elster! The area of the old village was located around the knight's estate in the region of today's rose garden and up the Kesselbach valley. The inhabitants were poor farmers who were obliged to pay interest and perform compulsory labor. Whether they were attacked in 1430 by the Hussites retreating to Bohemia who had before pillaged Oelsnitz and Plauen is not confirmed by documents. Also participation of the Elster farmers in the Farmers War cannot exactly be proven. It is, however, likely that also the Elster farmers met at the end of April 1525 «with the farmers of the southern country court Adorf at Land-wuest in a field camp». Elector Johann of Saxony personally held court from June 30 to July 1 of the same year in Plauen over «the rioters». All villages of the Vogtsberg office which probably included Elster were fined.

It is very likely that at this time the old Elster Village Church already existed. In the tradition even an «early mass and pilgrimage church» is mentioned. Standing alone on the church hill, it could have already existed before the settlement of the first Elster farmers. It is certain that Romanesque elements could be seen on the old secular building which was demolished in 1892. The small windows in the

romanische Rundbogenfenster. Außerdem wurde die beim Abriß erkennbare Grundrißdisposition als «romanisch» bezeichnet. Die Kirche insgesamt war auf Grund der vielen Um- und Anbauten ein Gemisch mehrerer Stilepochen.

Spätestens seit 1490 hatte die alte Kirche einen gotischen Flügelaltar, dessen Figuren Petrus und Paulus der Kirche den Namen «Peter-Pauls-Kirche» gaben. Diese geschnitzten Holzfiguren wurden in den späteren Barockaltar übernommen, wie aus alten Fotos hervorgeht. Heute kann man beide im Chorraum der neuen Trinitatiskirche bewundern. Auf ihrer Rückseite tragen sie die Inschrift «Hof 1490».

Die Dorfkirche «Peter und Paul» wurde damals vom Kaplan zu Adorf bedient. Es hatte also kein Geistlicher selbst seinen Sitz in Elster, sondern er kam für jede Amtshandlung nach Elster «herbeigeritten».

Seit der Christianisierung und Besiedelung hatte der Deutsche Ritterorden die Organisation von Kirche und Schule stabilisiert und ausgebaut. Geleitet wurde das «Deutsche Haus» in Adorf von einem «Comthur», der die geistliche Oberaufsicht führte. Der Pfarrer zu Adorf unterstützte ihn und der «Kaplan oder Diacon» saß zwar in Adorf, war aber in erster Linie für Elster zuständig.

Als 1529 eine Visitation zur Vorbereitung der Reformation in Adorf durchgeführt wurde, ist offenbar erwogen worden, Elster zur eigenständigen Pfarrei zu erheben. Das unterblieb aber, so daß der erste evangelische Pfarrer für Elster mit Einführung der Reformation 1533/34 weiter seinen Sitz in Adorf hatte. Es war der 1540 von Martin Luther ordinierte Michael Schädel, der wie alle weiteren evangelischen Geistlichen den Titel «Diacon zu Adorf und Prediger zu Elster» führte. Zwischen der «weltlichen und geistlichen Macht» spielte sich das Leben der «Urelsteraner» ab, das durch harte Arbeit (Frondienste) und ein heute unvorstellbares niedriges Lebensniveau gekennzeichnet war. Die kleinen Bohlenständerhäuschen, deren Bauart und Größe für die vorreformatorische Zeit in Elster typisch waren, vermitteln ein anschauliches Bild vom Lebensstil unserer Vorfahren.

Vom Dorf zum Staatsbad

Eine erste Untersuchung des Elsteraner «Dorfbrunnens», dem in den Elsterwiesen entspringenden Säuerling, der heutigen Moritzquelle, fand bereits 1538 statt. Das geht aus einem Bericht des Amtsschössers auf Schloß Vogtsberg bei Oelsnitz hervor. Da die Untersuchung zum Zwecke der Salzgewinnung erfolgte, mußte sie ohne Ergebnis bleiben. Anderen Angaben zufolge datiert diese erste Quellenanalyse schon von 1531.

Der 1546/47 wütende Schmalkaldische Krieg scheint Elster nicht, wohl aber Adorf und Markneukirchen erreicht zu haben. 1556 wurde Elster mit Adorf und dem übrigen, heute sächsischen Vogtland von Heinrich VI., Graf von Reuß und Plauen, an den Kurfürsten August von Sachsen verpfändet und am 15.10.1564 endgültig an Sachsen abgetreten.

Am 14. Juni 1556 läßt Thomas Grüner, Schulmeister in Elster, in Adorf eine Tochter taufen. Damit ist die erste urkundliche Erwähnung eines Schuldienstes in Elster erfolgt. Aus dem Jahr 1616 findet sich in den Akten der Superintendentur Oelsnitz ein weiterer Nachweis über den Schuldienst im Ort. In den Jahren 1632/33 wird Elster erstmals vom Dreißigjährigen Krieg heimgesucht. Aus dieser Zeit stammt wohl auch die Schwedenschanze am Brunnenberg.

Als 1644 die Holkschen Truppen zum zweiten Mal kommen, kann in der Elsteraner Dorfkirche vom 2. bis 19. Sonntag nach Trinitatis kein Gottesdienst stattfinden, weil sie verwüstet ist.

lower part of the tower were, for example, Romanesque round arched windows. Furthermore, the disposition of the floorplan which became obvious after the demolition was called «Romanesque». The church as a whole was, due to the many alterations and additional buildings, a mixture of several styles.

At least since 1490 the old church had a Gothic winged altarpiece whose statues of Peter and Paul gave the church the name «Peter-Paul's Church». These carved wooden figures were moved into the later Baroque altar as can be seen in old photographs. Today both can be admired in the choir room of the new Trinitatis (Trinity) Church. On the rear side of the figures is the inscription «Hof 1490».

The village church «Peter and Paul» was at that time serviced by the Curate of Adorf. No priest had his seat in Elster but the curate «rode over» to Elster for every official act.

Since the Christianization and settlement the Teutonic Order had stabilized and extended the organization of church and school. The «German House» was guided in Adorf by a «Comthur» who was the clerical supervisor. The priest of Adorf supported him and although the «curate or deacon» was seated in Adorf, he was primarily responsible for Elster.

When in 1529 a visitation was carried out in order to prepare for the Reformation in Adorf, it was obviously considered to make Elster an independent parish. But this was not done and so the first Protestant minister for Elster continued to have his seat in Adorf after the introduction of the Reformation in 1533-34. It was Michael Schaedel who was ordained by Martin Luther in 1540 and who, similar to other Protestant clergymen, held the title «Deacon of Adorf and Preacher of Elster».

Between the «mundane and secular powers» the life of the «original people of Elster» took place, which was characterized by hard work (compulsory labor) and a low standard of living which is impossible to imagine today. The small houses built on planks whose building type and size were typical for the pre-Reformational period in Elster provide a descriptive picture of the lifestyle of our predecessors.

From Village to State Bath

A first examination of the Elster «village fountain» of the mineral spring, today's Moritz Spring, which has its origin in the Elster meadows already took place in 1538. This becomes obvious from a report of the official of Vogtsberg castle near Oelsnitz. Since the examination was performed for the purpose of salt exploitation, it had to remain without result. According to other data this first analysis of the spring even goes back to 1531.

The Smalkaldic War which raged in 1546-47 did not seem to have reached Elster but Adorf and Markneukirchen. In 1556 Elster was, together with Adorf and the remaining parts of today's Saxonian Vogtland, pawned by Heinrich VI, Court of Reuss and Plauen, to Elector August of Saxony and finally ceded to Saxony on October 15, 1564.

On June 14, 1556 Thomas Gruener, teacher in Elster, had his daughter baptized in Adorf. Thus school service in Elster is for the first time documented. In the files of the superintendent's office in Oelsnitz another piece of evidence about school service in the village from 1616 can be found. In the years 1632–33 Elster was for the first time affected by the Thirty Years War. The fortifications against the Swedes at the Brunnenberg Mountain probably date back to that time. When in 1644 the Swedish troops returned for the second time, no church service could take place in the Elster village church from the second until the 19th Sundays after Trinity, since the church had

Im Jahr 1669 nimmt der Plauener Arzt und Stadtphysikus Georg Leisner auf Geheiß des Wettiners Moritz von Sachsen-Zeitz (1656 bis 1681) die zweite Quellenuntersuchung vor. Das Ergebnis ist der bis heute vorhandene Bericht: «Acidularum Elistranarum Lympha/Das ist: Kurtzer Bericht Des Elster-Sauerlings». Dieser Quellenanalyse verdankt der Säuerling seinen heutigen Namen: «Moritz-Quelle».

Im Jahre 1709 erhielt der älteste Gasthof, auf dessen Platz heute das Kurhotel «Haus am See» (seit 1848 «Reichsverweser») steht, die «Real- und Schankgerechtigkeit». Möglich ist, daß der Gasthof «Zum Roten Ochsen» hieß. An ihm mag auf der alten Heer- und Handelsstraße, die vom Kirchberg kommend hier entlang ins Böhmische führte, mancher Landsknecht und Reitersmann nicht nur vorbeigezogen sein.

Später, als in den ärmlichen Schindelhäusern im «Kessel» tagein tagaus die ersten Webstühle klapperten, hielten die Elsteraner Hausweber hier ihre Innungsversammlungen ab. Zur gleichen Zeit, also 1709, wird eine erste bauliche Erneuerung des Elstersäuerlings erwähnt.

Aus dem Jahr 1724 stammt die Halbmeilensäule der kursächsischen Post, die neben dem Signum Augusts des Starken auch die Entfernung nach Adorf, Asch und Eger in Stunden anzeigt. 1982 restauriert, steht sie heute auf dem Kirchplatz. 1728 wurde die Dorfschule, das jetzige Kirchgemeindehaus, fertiggestellt. Sie dürfte damit das älteste unverändert erhaltene Gebäude von Bad Elster sein, weshalb sie mit dem schönen alten Torbogen unter Denkmalschutz steht.

Überlieferungen zufolge sollen 1734 Salzburger Emigranten, die wegen ihres protestantischen Glaubens verfolgt waren, durch Elster gezogen sein. Im Bayerischen Erbfolgekrieg 1778/79 war die Dorfkirche wieder betroffen: Das Kirchenornat wurde geraubt. 1789 erhielt die heutige Moritzquelle eine feste steinerne Fassung. Nach Steuerrat Trauer soll Johann Wolfgang von Goethe am 3. oder 4. Juli 1795 in Elster gewesen sein.

Der Anblick der neu gefaßten Moritzquelle soll Goethe zur Dichtung von «Hermann und Dorothea» inspiriert haben, weshalb dieses Stück später im Elsteraner Naturtheater oft aufgeführt worden ist. Dazu bemerkt Griebens Reiseführer «Bad Elster und Umgebung» aus dem Jahre 1928:

«Erwähnt sei hier noch, daß in neuester Zeit durch Steuerrat Trauer, Dresden, der Nachweis erbracht worden ist, daß Goethe in der Schilderung seiner Dichtung «Hermann und Dorothea» Adorf und Elster vor Augen gehabt hat, ein Landstädtchen und ein in der Nähe gelegenes Dorf mit einem Sauerbrunnen – «herrlichem Wasser», säuerlich war's und erquicklich, gesund zu trinken den Menschen» –. Goethe war dreimal im oberen Vogtland. Am 3. Juli 1795 übernachtete er auf der Durchreise nach Karlsbad in Adorf im Posthaus des Reichskonsulenten und Postmeisters Pinder, der zugleich Gerichtsdirektor von Elster war. Goethe beschäftigte sich damals schon mit dem Stoff, den er im folgenden Jahr in «Hermann und Dorothea» bearbeitete. Nun war es Tatsache, daß im Juli 1732 ein Zug vertriebener Salzburger, der von Asch nach Sachsen zog, in dem Dorf Elster über Nacht gerastet hatte. Da Pinder die Aufsicht über die Mineralquellen des oberen Vogtlandes hatte, so ist es sehr wahrscheinlich, daß Goethe Elster in Begleitung Pinders aufsuchte, erst zu Fuß auf dem «abkürzenden Fußweg», dann zu Wagen! In alten Akten der Badedirektion Elster ist der «Sauerbrunnen» genau beschrieben und abgebildet, wie Goethe ihn in seinem Gedicht schildert. Die Badedirektion hat den Brunnen in der von Goethe beschriebenen Weise erneuern und mit einer Gedenktafel versehen lassen. Er befindet sich nahe der Moritzquelle und wurde in Verbindung mit einem Festspiel am 9. Juli 1911 feierlich enthüllt.»

Die dritte Untersuchung des Elstersäuerlings erfolgte 1799 und war schon eine wissenschaftlich exakte Analyse von Prof. Wilhelm Lampadius, Bergakademie Freiberg.

Die alte Elsteraner Dorfkirche «St. Peter und Paul» mit Scule im Jahre 1875.
The old Elster village church St. Peter and Paul with school in 1875.

been devastated. In 1669 the Plauen physician and town doctor Georg Leisner submitted upon request of the Wettin Moritz of Saxony-Zeitz (1656-1681) the second spring examination. The result was a report which still exists today: «Acidularum Elistranarum Lympha/that is: short report on the Elster mineral water». The mineral spring owes its present name: «Moritz Spring» to this spring analysis.

In 1709 the oldest inn at the place of which the resort hotel «Haus am See» (House on the Lake) is located today received its excise license. It is possible that the inn was called «Zum Roten Ochsen» (Way to the Red Ox). There, many a mercenary or horseman on the old troop and trade road, which coming from the Kirchberg Mountain passed here on its way into Bohemia, may not only have passed. Later when in the poor shingled houses in the «kettle» the first looms were rattling continuously, the Elster home weavers held their guild meetings there. At the same time, that is in 1709, the first constructional renovation of the Elster mineral spring is mentioned.

The half mile column of the post of the electorate of Saxony, which next to the signature of August the Strong also shows the distances to Adorf, Asch and Eger in hours, dates back to 1724. It was restored in 1982 and is today located on the Kirchplatz (church square). In 1728 the village school, today's church community house, was completed. It is probably the oldest building of Bad Elster which has been pre-

1806/07 wechselte das Rittergut nach fast 400 Jahren aus dem Besitz der Familie von Zedtwitz an den Kaufmann Joh. Chr. Wolfrum aus Hof. Im Jahr 1806 wird eine Glashütte auf der alten Schäferei des Rittergutes erwähnt. Sie gehörte dem Kaufmann Müller aus Auerbach und soll gutes Fensterglas geliefert haben. Schon nach wenigen Jahren brannte sie ab und wurde nicht wieder aufgebaut. Noch lange hielt sich für eine Anzahl dort gelegener Häuser die Bezeichnung «Glashütte». 1807 wird das »Gerichtshaus», das heutige Kurheim Haus «Linde» umgebaut. Es liegt gleichfalls auf dem Gelände der alten Schäferei, wofür der alte Name des darunter im Park gelegenen «Lindenteiches» spricht, der früher als «Schafteich» bekannt war.

Als 1810 das Flußbett der Elster umgelegt wird, entdeckt man die Marienquelle. In erster Linie äußere Umstände, weniger die Erkenntnis des gesundheitsspendenden Wertes dieses Naturschatzes, diktieren deren Nutzung. Eine Mißernte, die im gesamten oberen Vogtland zu einer Hungersnot führt, veranlaßt 1818 den Markneukirchner Stadtdirektor Staudinger zur Anordnung der Abgabe von Bädern in Zelten.

1819 entstand ein hölzerner Badeschuppen mit einigen Badestuben. Bereits 100 Badegäste wurden registriert. 1835 bildete sich ein «Verein patriotisch gesinnter Männer zur Emporbringung des Elsterbrunnens» unter Führung des Adorfer Bürgermeisters Todt. Zugleich entsteht eine Aktiengesellschaft zum Betrieb der Badeanlagen, Elster beginnt zu wachsen. 1843 wird die Adorfer Landstraße fertig und Elster hat 84 Häuser und 1100 Einwohner. Am 25. Juni 1848 eröffnete Dr. med. Robert Flechsig als Bade- und Brunnenarzt feierlich die erste offizielle Badesaison des Königlich-Sächsischen Staatsbades Elster. Damit ist Bad Elster einer der ältesten Kurorte Deutschlands, und der König hatte endlich ein eigenes Kurbad in Sachsen.

Die «Eremitage», Schutzhütte am Brunnenberg, 1875.
The «Eremitage» (Hermitage) refuge on the Brunnenberg Mountain in 1875.

served in its unaltered form. Therefore it was classified together with the beautiful old archway as a national monument.

Tradition has it that in 1732 emigrants from Salzburg, who were persecuted because of their Protestant belief, passed through Elster. The Bavarian War of Succession of 1778–79 again affected the village church: the ecclesiastical vestments were stolen. In 1789 today's Moritz Spring was given a firm stone border. According to tax counselor Trauer, Johann Wolfgang von Goethe is believed to have been in Elster on July 3 or 4, 1795. The site of the newly bordered Moritz Spring is said to have inspired Goethe to his work «Hermann and Dorothea» which is why this play was later often performed at the Elster Nature Theater. Grieben's tour guide «Bad Elster and Surroundings» from 1928 observes the following:

«It shall be mentioned that recently evidence has been shown by tax counselor Trauer of Dresden that Goethe in his description of his play 'Hermann and Dorothea' had Adorf and Elster in mind, a country town and a nearby village with a mineral fountain – 'with marvelous water', 'which was tart and refreshing and a healthy beverage for people'. Goethe was three times in the Upper Vogtland. On July 3, 1795 he spent the night in transit to Karlsbad in Adorf in the post house of the Imperial counselor and postmaster Pinder who was at the same time Court Director of Elster. Already at that time Goethe was occupied with the plot which he them used in the following year in 'Hermann and Dorothea'. It was a fact that in July 1732 a group of persecuted people from Salzburg who moved from Asch to Saxony had spent the night in the village of Elster. Since Pinder supervised the mineral springs of the Upper Vogtland, it is very likely that Goethe visited Elster in Pinder's company first on foot via a 'short cutting footpath', then by cart! In the old files of the bath administration of Elster the 'mineral fountain' is precisely described and pictured as Goethe depicts it in his poem. The bath administration had the fountain restored in the manner described by Goethe and equipped it with a memorial plaque. It is located close to the mineral spring and was solemnly unveiled in connection with a festival on July 9, 1911.»

The third examination of the Elster mineral spring was done in 1799 and was already a scientifically exact analysis by Professor Wilhelm Lampadius of the Bergakademie Freiberg.

In 1806–07 the knight's estate was transferred after almost 400 years from the ownership of the von Zedtwitz family to the merchant Joh.Chr. Wolfrum from Hof. In 1806 a glass factory on the old sheep farm of the knight's estate is mentioned. It belonged to the merchant Mueller from Auerbach and is said to have provided good window glass. It burned down after only a few years and was not rebuilt. For a long time some houses located there were still referred to as «glass factory». In 1807 the «court house», today's spa house in the «Linde» house, was rebuilt. It is as well located in the area of the old sheep farm which is attested to by the old name of the «Linden Pond» below in the park which used to be known as «sheep pond».

In 1810 the bed of the Elster River was redirected and the Marien Spring was discovered. Its exploitation was primarily dictated by external circumstances, less by the insight into the wholesome value of this natural treasure. A crop failure which caused a famine in the entire Upper Vogtland made the town director Staudinger of Markneukirchen order bathing in tents in 1818.

In 1819 a wooden bath cabana with some bathing rooms came into being. Already 100 bath guests were registered. Elster began to grow. In 1843 the Adorf road was completed and Elster had 84 houses and 1,100 inhabitants. In 1847 the medical doctor Robert Flechsig came to Elster in order to create the preconditions for a regulated bath operation. On June 25, 1848 he as bath and fountain doctor solemnly opened the first official bathing season of the Royal Saxonian State Bath Elster. Thus Bad Elster became one of the oldest spas in Germany and the king finally had his own health resort in Saxony.

Elster wird Weltbad

Nachdem Elster Königlich-Sächsisches Staatsbad geworden war, ging die Umgestaltung besonders des alten Badeplatzes zügig voran. Bis 1850/51 waren Straßen, Promenaden und Parkanlagen in diesem zentralen Bereich angelegt, und man konnte auch äußerlich von einem Kurbad reden. Weiterhin wurde 1851 die Salzquelle entdeckt und 1852 das Badehaus fertiggestellt. Auch kulturell bot Elster schon in den Anfängen viel. Bereits 1818 begann Johann Christoph Hilf (1783–1885) mit der «Curmusik». Auf Betreiben des Gerichtsdirektors Staudinger brachte er ein kleines Orchester zusammen und gründete damit die Kurkapelle.

Am 7. September 1851 wird Gustav Kuhn als erster Pfarrer der seitdem eigenständigen Pfarrei (Bad) Elster eingeführt. So kann man erst seit 1851 von der juristisch selbständigen Kirchgemeinde (Bad) Elster reden. Bis 1859 gab es auch nur einen einzigen Lehrer für die Elsteraner Schüler, der gleichzeitig Kantor war. Erst dann wurde ein zweiter Lehrer angestellt.

Neben dem im oberen Vogtland nicht sehr ertragreichen Ackerbau betrieben die Elsteraner vor dem Aufblühen des Kurbetriebes vor allem die Hausweberei. Fast in jedem der kleinen Elsteraner Häuser stand damals ein Webstuhl. 1859, zur «Schillerfeier» traten die Hausweber zum letzten Mal als geschlossene Innung mit einer Fahne an die Öffentlichkeit. Wesentlich für die Entwicklung des Königlich-Sächsischen Staatsbades war die Eröffnung der Eisenbahnlinie Herlasgrün-Oelsnitz-Eger im Jahre 1865. Damit war eine erhebliche Verbesserung der Reisebedingungen für die Kurgäste gegeben. Aber auch der Güterverkehr wurde dadurch erleichtert. Ebenso wichtig erscheint der Ankauf des Rittergutes durch den sächsischen Staat im gleichen Jahr, eine grundlegende Voraussetzung für die weitere Umgestaltung Elsters zum Kurbad.

Da der Kurbetrieb sich aber nur in den Sommermonaten abspielte, waren die Einwohner weiter auch auf die Ausübung anderer Gewerbe angewiesen. So hatte sich bis 1871 die Samtweberei auf modernen Webstühlen durchgesetzt. Die in den Häusern hergestellten Waren

Elster Becomes a World Bath

After Elster had become Royal Saxonian State Bath, the restoration especially of the old bath site proceeded rapidly. By 1850-51 roads, promenades and park facilities had been established in this central area and it could be called a spa also from its outward appearance. Furthermore, the salt spring was discovered in 1851 and the bath house was completed in 1852. Elster from the beginning also offered a variety of cultural activities. Johann Christoph Hilf (1783-1885) began the «spa music» already in 1818. Upon the initiative of the court director Staudinger he formed a small orchestra and thus founded the spa band.

On September 7, 1851 Gustav Kuhn was introduced as the first clergyman of the (Bad) Elster parish which has been independent ever since. Thus one can only speak about a legally independent church community of (Bad) Elster since 1851. Up to 1859 there was only one teacher for the Elster pupils who was cantor at the same time. Only then was a second teacher hired.

Apart from agriculture which was not very productive in the Upper Vogtland, the Elster people engaged predominantly in home weaving before the flourishing of the spa operation. There was a loom in almost every one of the small Elster houses at that time. In 1859 on the occasion of the «Schiller Celebration» the home weavers appeared in public for the first time as uniform guild with their own flag.

The opening of the railway line Herlasgruen-Oelsnitz-Eger in 1865 was essential for the development of the Royal Saxonian State Bath. Thus a considerable improvement in travel conditions for the guests of the health resort was provided. Also the transport of goods was thereby facilitated. The purchase of the knight's estate by the Saxonian State in the same year was as important and formed a basic prerequisite for the further redesign of Elster into a health resort.

Since the spa operation, however, was limited to the summer months, the inhabitants continued to rely on the performance of other trades. By 1871 velvet weaving on modern looms had proliferated. The goods manufactured in the houses had to be delivered

11

mußten an Verleger in Asch, Adorf und Roßbach ausgeliefert werden. 1875 soll ein Unternehmer direkt in Elster mit 70 Webstühlen gearbeitet haben.

1873 gibt es bereits acht Mineralquellen. Erst 1875 erhält das Königlich-Sächsische Staatsbad Elster vom Deutschen Bäderverband offiziell das Recht, sich «Bad» Elster zu nennen.

Als neue Schule wurde 1876 das heutige Gebäude 2 der Elsteraner Schule am Kirchplatz seiner Bestimmung übergeben. Im Jahr 1877 wird der neue Friedhof mit Kapelle geweiht. Im gleichen Jahr war die Kreuzkapelle am Brunnenberg fertig, in der heute wieder Waldgottesdienste stattfinden, was 1959 verboten worden war.

In nur zwei Jahren (1888–1890) wurde das Kurhaus errichtet. Zur Gestaltung der davor liegenden Parkanlagen wurde Paul Schindel nach Bad Elster gerufen. In den Folgejahren prägte er mit der Anlage der Elsteraner Parks maßgeblich das Ortsbild. Am 1.11.1889 erfolgte die Grundsteinlegung für die neue Stadtkirche; Bauherr war Pfarrer Freiherr von Bernewitz. Nach genau zwei Jahren und sieben Monaten wurde sie am 1. Juni 1892 als ev.-luth. Kirche auf den Namen der heiligen Dreieinigkeit – St. Trinitatis geweiht. Ein paar Monate standen beide Kirchen noch nebeneinander, bis die alte Dorfkirche abgerissen wurde.

1893–1895 wurde im Bereich des heutigen Gondelteiches Moor gestochen und mit Hilfe einer Elektrobahn zum Moorhof am Badehaus gefahren. Schon seit 1898 lieferte das Fernheizwerk Dampf zur Wärmeversorgung des Kurbades.

Seit Mitte des 19. Jahrhunderts erfolgte die Aufforstung der Bad Elster umgebenden Berge. Für die Anlage der Waldflächen hatte von 1879–1891 Oberforstmeister Heinrich August von Cotta, zu dessen Forstgebiet mit Sitz in Auerbach auch Bad Elster gehörte, die Verantwortung. Nach ihm wurde die Cotta-Terrasse am Brunnenberg benannt. Forstmeister von Römer leitete 1885–1910 den Forstbetrieb. Die Römerhütte am Arnsgrüner Kirchsteig trägt noch heute seinen Namen.

Wesentlichen Einfluß auf die Entwicklung Bad Elsters übte der Arzt und Wissenschaftler Dr. med. Paul Köhler seit 1903 aus. In der Prof.-Paul-Köhler-Straße liegen das von ihm gegründete Sanatorium und seine letzte Ruhestätte.

1907 brannte der alte «Wettiner Hof» ab. An seiner Stelle wurde

to dealers in Asch, Adorf and Rossbach. In 1875 an entrepreneur is believed to have worked with 70 looms in Elster.

In 1873 there were already eight mineral springs. Only in 1875 was the Royal Saxonian State Bath Elster officially granted the right to call itself «Bad» Elster by the German Bath Association.

In 1876 today's building 2 of the Elster school was opened as new school at Kirchplatz (church square). In 1877 the new cemetery with its chapel was consecrated. In the same year the Kreuzkapelle (cross chapel) at Brunnenberg Mountain was completed where once again today forest worship services again take place which had been forbidden in 1959.

In only two years (1888-1890) the spa house was established. Paul Schindel was called to Bad Elster to design the park facilities in front of it. In the following years he considerably marked the appearance of the village with the establishment of the Elster Park.

On November 1, 1889 the foundation stone was laid for the new town church. The builder was the priest Baron of Bernewitz. After exactly two years and seven months it was consecrated on June 1, 1892 as Protestant church with the name of the Holy Trinity, St. Trinitatis. For a few months both churches stood next to one another until the old village church was demolished.

In 1893 to 1895 peat was cut in the area of today's gondola pond and brought to the peat yard at the spa house with the help of an electric railway. The long distance heating plant provided steam for the health resort already since 1898.

Since the middle of the 19th century the mountains surrounding Bad Elster were reforested. District forest officer Heinrich of Cotta who was seated in Auerbach and whose forest area also included Bad Elster was responsible for the planting of the wooded areas from 1879 to 1891. The Cotta Terrace on Brunnenberg Mountain was named for him. Forest Officer von Roemer was in charge of forest operations from 1885 to 1910. The Roemer cabin at Arnsgruen Kirchsteig bears his name still today.

The physician and scientist Dr. Paul Koehler exerted considerable influence on the development of Bad Elster. The sanatorium founded by him and his place of final rest are located on Professor-Paul-Koehler Street.

In 1907 the old Wettin Court burned down. In its place the new

das neue Palasthotel «Wettiner Hof» errichtet. Der westliche Flügel des Badehauses, das «Albertbad», wurde 1908 fertig. In ihm befindet sich bis heute die königliche Badezelle, die sich durch besonders wertvolle Ausstattung auszeichnet.

Besonders der letzte sächsische König Friedrich August III. (Regierungszeit vom 15.10.1904–13.11.1918) hat sie oft und gern aufgesucht, allerdings nicht als Kurpatient. Seine Besuche in Bad Elster sind im Kurregister in den Jahren von 1914 bis 1918 lückenlos erfaßt. Zumeist Ende April, also vor Beginn der Kursaison, kam der König für wenige Tage nach Bad Elster. Auf dem Bahnhof rollte dann am Abend sein Salonwagen ein, und der Bahnhofsvorsteher mußte Oberförster Oeser informieren, damit der sich vor Morgengrauen einfinde. Gemeinsam mit Hof-Jägermeister von Arnim ging es dann auf Auerhahnjagd, später folgte ein Besuch der königlichen Badezelle, und abends wurde gekegelt. In seinem «geliebten Bad Elster» suchte und fand der als volksverbundener Mann beliebte König so immer einige Stunden Erholung und Entspannung.

1910 wurde das Gemeindeamt, das heutige Rathaus gebaut. Die Weihe der katholischen Kirche «St. Elisabeth» am Stadion erfolgte 1913. Durch König Friedrich August III. wurde 1914 das Kurtheater eröffnet. Schon vorher hatte es in Bad Elster einen Theaterbau gegeben. Das «Alberttheater» war ein Fachwerkbau und lag neben dem Haus «Sachsengrün» unterhalb des «Schillergartens».

Nach dem Ersten Weltkrieg wurden 1919–1923 die Moortaschen angelegt. In ihnen wird bis heute das abgebadete Moor mindestens 10 Jahre zwischengelagert und nach seiner Regenerierung dem Frischmoor beigemischt. «Moor-Recycling» ist also keine Erfindung unserer Tage, sondern wird in Bad Elster schon über viele Jahrzehnte praktiziert. In den Jahren 1923, 1925 und 1935 wurden die Sprudelquellen 1 und 2 erbohrt und gefaßt. 1927 ist das Badehaus in seiner heutigen Form fertiggestellt. Das Stadion wurde 1928–1931 angelegt und gehört seither zu den schönsten Stadien im Vogtland.

Die Wandelhalle, aus Postelwitzer Elbsandstein im Bauhausstil errichtet, wurde 1929 fertig. In den Jahren 1933–1934 gestaltet man den Badeplatz mit Kolonnaden, Marienquelle und Badecafe zu seiner heutigen Form um. 1936 erhielt Bad Elster Stadtrecht und ist seitdem die südlichste Stadt Sachsens. Vorher konnte Markneukirchen diesen «Titel» beanspruchen.

palace hotel «Wettiner Hof» was established. The west wing of the bath house, the «Albertbad» was completed in 1908. Up to the present day it houses the royal bath cabana which excels by its particularly valuable fixtures.

Especially the last Saxonian King Friedrich August III (time of rule from October 15, 1904 to November 13, 1918) liked to visit it often, although not as a health resort patient. His visits to Bad Elster were recorded without gaps in the spa register in the years from 1914 to 1918. The king came for a few days to Bad Elster, usually at the end of April which was also the beginning of the spa season. In the evening his precious car would roll into the railway station and the stationmaster had to inform Forest Officer Oeser so that he would show up at the break of dawn. Together with Spa Director von Alberti and Court Hunting Master von Arnim he chased capercaillie; the hunt was followed by a visit to the royal bath cabana and in the evening they all went bowling. In his «beloved Bad Elster» the king who was popular as a man close to the people always sought and found a few hours of relaxation and recreation.

In 1910 the community office, today's town hall, was built. The consecration of the Catholic church «St. Elisabeth» at the stadium was performed in 1913. In 1914 the spa theater was reopened by King Friedrich August III. Already before then there had been a theater building in Bad Elster. The «Albert Theater» was a half-timbered building located next to the «Sachsengruen» house below the Schiller Garden.

After World War I the mud pits were established from 1919 to 1923. There the used mud has been until now deposited for at least ten years and after its regeneration mixed with fresh mud. «Mud recycling» is not an invention of our days, but has been practiced in Bad Elster for many decades. In the years 1923, 1925 and 1935 the mineral springs 1 and 2 were drilled and lined. In 1927 the bath house was completed in its present form. The stadium was established from 1928 to 1931 and has ever since been among the most beautiful stadia in Vogtland.

The pump house erected from Postelwitz Elbe sandstone in the Bauhaus style was completed in 1929. In the years 1933-34 the bath site was decorated with colonnades, the Marien Spring and the bath cafe in its present form. In 1936 Bad Elster was granted the status of

Die Zeit des Dritten Reiches hinterläßt auch in Bad Elster ihre Spuren. Grundvoraussetzung für einen Kuraufenthalt ist nicht das Krankheitsbild oder der Geldbeutel, sondern deutsche Reinrassigkeit. So wurden dem Weltbad andere, tiefere Wunden geschlagen als durch den Krieg, den es äußerlich unbeschadet überstand.

1947 beschloß der Sächsische Landtag ein «Gesetz zur Sicherstellung von Kurbädern», und Bad Elster wurde zum «Bad der Werktätigen». Ein neuer Entwicklungsabschnitt beginnt.

Im Jahr 1949, wenige Monate nach der 100-Jahrfeier des Sächsischen Staatsbades, entstand als erster Bau nach dem Krieg die «Kurpoliklinik», zuletzt als «Zentrale Diagnostik» betrieben. Das Naturtheater, oberhalb der Gaststätte «Waldquelle» gelegen, blieb noch bis 1952 in Betrieb. Schillers «Wilhelm Tell» und Shakespeares «Was ihr wollt» gehörten zu den letzten Aufführungen. Ebenfalls in den 50er Jahren fand das letzte große Brunnenfest statt.

Nach einem starken Hochwasser der Weißen Elster mußte 1956 die Marienquelle vollständig neu gefaßt werden. Ihre innere Gestaltung von der Brunnenschale bis zur Kuppelbeleuchtung stammt also aus dieser Zeit. Im gleichen Jahr sowie 1957 wurden die Sprudelquellen 3 und 4 erbohrt und gefaßt.

Die Gründung des Forschungsinstitutes für Balneologie und Kurortwissenschaft als zweites Elsteraner Institut erfolgte ebenfalls 1957.

1982 wurde der Sanatoriumskomplex in Betrieb genommen. Der Vorgang dieses Neubaus wurde begleitet vom Verfall des ehemaligen prachtvollen Palasthotels «Wettiner Hof», einem Wahrzeichen der Stadt. Es steht heute zur Rekonstruktion. 1989 wurde das neue «Haus am See» als eine moderne, allen Ansprüchen genügende Sanatoriumseinrichtung eingeweiht. Es befindet sich an der Stelle des ältesten, 1709 erstmals erwähnten Gasthofs.

Abgesehen von wenigen Eingriffen dieser Art sind die für Identität und Ausstrahlung Bad Elsters unverzichtbaren, historisch gewachsenen Strukturen in ihrer Gesamtheit weitgehend erhalten.

a town and has ever since been the southernmost town of Saxony. Prior to that Markneukirchen could lay claim to this «title».

The period of the Third Reich also left its traces in Bad Elster. The basic precondition for a stay in the health resort was not the state of health or the size of purse but German purity of race. Thus the world bath was administered different deeper wounds than through the war which it survived outwardly undamaged.

In 1947 the Saxonian parliament passed a «law in order to secure health resorts» and Bad Elster became a «bath for the working class». A new chapter in its development began.

In 1949 a few months after the 100th anniversary of the Saxonian state bath, the «health resort dispensary» which was in the end operated as «central diagnostics» was erected as the first new building after the war. The nature theater above the inn «Waldquelle» (forest spring) continued its operation until 1952. Schiller's «William Tell» and Shakespeare's «As You Like It» were among the last performances. The last great fountain festival also took place in the 1950's.

After a considerable inundation of the Weisse Elster River, the Marien Spring had to be completely relined in 1956. Its inner design from the fountain bowl to the dome lighting also dates back to this period. In the same year as well as in 1957 the mineral springs 3 and 4 were drilled and lined.

In 1982 the sanatorium complex began its operation. The establishment of this new building was accompanied by the decay of the former splendid palace hotel «Wettiner Hof», a landmark of the town. It is available for reconstruction today. In 1989 the new «Haus am See» (house on the lake) was inaugurated as a modern sanatorium facility satisfying all requirements. It is located at the site of the oldest inn, which was mentioned for the first time in 1709.

Except for a few interferences of this kind, the historically grown structures which are indispensable for the identity and aura of Bad Elster have largely been preserved in their entirety.

Baugeschichte und Ortsgestaltung

In kaum einem Bade- und Kurort sind Ortskern, Kureinrichtungen, Kurpark und Landschaft derartig günstig zu einem Ensemble verschmolzen wie in Bad Elster. Der interessierte Gast wird recht bald erkennen, daß der Faktor Kur die Gestaltung dieser Stadt maßgeblich beeinflußt hat. Die Handschriften der Bauherren und Stadtväter seit der Gründung des Staatsbades 1848 bezeugen heute deren großen Sachverstand und hohes Einfühlungsvermögen. In Bad Elster findet man kaum den oft so schmerzhaften Bruch, den einander ablösende Baustile hinterlassen. Dieser Ort ist ein Zeugnis dafür, daß verschiedene Generationen sehr wohl ein Werk vollbringen können; Voraussetzung ist einzig und allein das gemeinsame Ziel. Noch in der ersten Hälfte des vergangenen Jahrhunderts werden die Einwohner des kleinen verschlafenen Dörfchens Elster der zunehmenden Einflußnahme durch die Sächsische Staatsregierung mit verhaltener Skepsis gegenüber gestanden haben. Inzwischen weiß jeder, daß die direkte Verbindung zur Residenzstadt Dresden ein Segen für den Ort war. Denn nur durch diese Verbindung konnten erstklassige Fachleute gewonnen werden. Außerdem war damit auch eine weit voraus schauende Grundstückspolitik verbunden. Heute ist Bad Elster ein idyllischer Villenort in einer unverwechselbaren wunderbaren Landschaft. Das eingangs geschilderte Ensemble ist in seiner Gesamtheit unter Denkmalschutz gestellt.

Schon aus weiter Ferne ist die 54 m hohe nadelartige Kirchturmspitze zu sehen. Die 1892 geweihte St. Trinitatiskirche von Bad Elster ist ein Werk des Dresdner Architekten Schramm. Mit ihren historistischen Schmuckelementen erinnert sie an einen frühgotischen Bau. Ein für Kirchen des ausgehenden 19. Jahrhunderts typischer Stil. Der Vorgängerbau, der noch bis zur Fertigstellung des Neubaus direkt daneben gestanden hat, war eine kleinere Dorfkirche mit barocker Turmhaube. An diese sehr alte, über die Jahrhunderte gewachsene Peter-Pauls-Kirche erinnern nur noch die gotischen Holzplastiken des Schnitzaltars aus dem Jahre 1490. Diese Kirche war bereits in den alten Meilenblättern verzeichnet. Der Überlieferung nach könnte es eine Frühmeß- und Wallfahrtskirche gewesen sein. Der Abriß des noch bis 1892 genutzten Gotteshauses zeugt von der rasanten Entwicklung des Badeortes in der 2. Hälfte des vergangenen Jahrhunderts.

Schon um 1850 setzte eine rege Bautätigkeit ein. Das noch heute zum Ensemble des Badeplatzes gehörende Badehaus wurde bereits 1852 in Betrieb genommen. In dieser Zeit erfolgte auch der Bau einer Trinkhalle für die drei am Fuße des Brunnenberges gelegenen Quellen, die Marienquelle, die Albertquelle und die Königsquelle. Vor der Trinkhalle befand sich eine sogenannte Wandelbahn mit Geschäften und Informationseinrichtungen. Ein Holzfachwerkbau, in Form und Bauweise ähnlich dem in den Jahren 1860/61 vollendeten Bau der Trinkhallen über der Salz- und Moritzquelle. Gegenüber dem Badehaus, auf der Südseite des Badeplatzes, wurde 1867/68 ein Kaffee-Salon errichtet. Ihm zur Seite entstand 1869 eine Musikhalle. Damit war die Bebauung des Badeplatzes vorerst abgeschlossen. In sehr kurzer Zeit war ein Kurzentrum entstanden, das über viele Jahre hinweg als Rahmen für das Badeleben in Bad Elster dienen sollte. Das Badehaus hingegen drohte ständig aus den Nähten zu platzen. In Anbetracht des steigenden Bedarfs wurde es immer wieder umgebaut und vergrößert. Bereits 1856 wurde ein erster Anbau errichtet. Der so geschlossen wirkende Gebäudekomplex entstand in sieben Jahrzehnten. In ihm sind die verschiedensten Architekturstile und Auffassungen vereint. Mit der etwas versteckt liegenden Kuppelhalle des Badehaus-Waldflügels besitzt Bad Elster ein Kleinod, das in der Umgebung seinesgleichen sucht. Die von Landbaumeister Waldow in den Jahren 1882/83 geschaffene Halle birgt ein kostbares Original künstlerischer Innenraumdekoration. Das Deckengemälde und die plastischen Re-

Construction History and Town Design

There is hardly a bath and health resort whose town center spa facilities, spa park and landscape have as favorabl merged into an ensemble as in Bad Elster. The spa factor has considerably influenced the design of this town. The handwritings of the builders and city fathers since the foundation of the state bath in 1848 testify to their great insight and sensitivity. In Bad Elster one hardly encounters the often so painful break left by architecture styles succeeding one another. This place is witness to the fact that various generations are very well able to complete a work; the only prerequisite is their common objective. After the first half of the last century the inhabitants of the small sleepy village of Elster were probably slightly skeptical towards the increasing influence of the Saxonian state government. Meanwhile everyone was aware of the fact that the direct connection to the royal residence town of Dresden was a blessing for it. Because first class experts could be attracted. Furthermore it was also linked to a visionary real estate policy. Today Bad Elster is an idyllic fashionable residential town in an unmistakably wonderful landscape. The previously mentioned ensemble has in its entirety been declared a national treasure

Already from a distance the 54 meter (177 foot) high needle-like church spire can be seen. The St. Trinitatis Church of Bad Elster which was consecrated on June 1, 1892 is the work of the Dresden architect Schramm. With its historical decorative elements it reminds one of an early Gothic structure, typical of churches at the end of the 19th century. Its predecessor, which was situated directly next to it until the completion of the new building, was a smaller village church with a Baroque tower cupola. We are only reminded of this ancient Peter-Paul's Church which had grown over the centuries by the Gothic wooden sculptures of the carved altar from 1490. This church was already mentioned in the old mile sheets. According to tradition it may have been an early mass and pilgrimage church. The demolition of this house of worship which was still used until 1892 testifies to the rapid development of the bath town in the second half of the last century.

Already in 1850 building activities increased. The bath house, which belongs to the ensemble of the bath site still today, began operation already in 1852. At that time also the construction of the drinking hall for the three springs situated at the foot of the Brunnenberg Mountain, the Marien Spring, the Albert Spring and the King's Spring was completed. In front of the drinking hall there was a so-called walking area with stores and information facilities. It was a wooden half-timbered building completed in 1860-61 whose form and architectural style were similar to the construction of the drinking halls above the Salt and Moritz Spring. Opposite the bath house on the south side of the bath site a coffee shop was built in 1867–68. In 1869 a music hall was erected next to it. Thus the architectural design of the bath site was for a while completed. Within a very short time a health spa center had come into being which was to serve for many years as a framework for the bath life in Bad Elster. The bath house, however, constantly threatened to burst. In view of the increasing demand it was repeatedly remodeled and enlarged. Already in 1856 a first extension was built. The building complex which provides such a uniform impression developed over seven decades. It unifies the most varied architectural styles and opinions. With the dome hall of the forest wing of the bath house, which is located in a somewhat hidden location, Bad Elster owns a gem unsurpassed in the area. The hall, created by country builder Waldow in the years 1882-83, accommodates a precious original of artistic interior design. The painting on the ceiling and the plastique reliefs were recently restored. The style of the works is reminiscent of the Semper Opera in Dresden.

Der Badeplatz nach 1856.   *The bath site after 1856.*

liefs wurden jüngst von Restauratoren gereinigt. Die Arbeiten erinnern in ihrem Stil an die Semperoper in Dresden.

Im Gegensatz zur äußerlich doch recht zurückhaltenden Kuppelhalle des Waldflügels wird das Ortsbild durch die an der Badstraße gelegene Front des Badehauses recht eindrucksvoll geprägt. Die Alberthalle mit ihren zwei Seitenflügeln, die von den Architekten Schilling & Graebener in Zusammenarbeit mit der königlichen Baudirektion, Oberbaurat Reh, geschaffen wurde, läßt alle anderen Teile des Gebäudekomplexes in den Hintergrund treten. Und das zu recht, denn das im wesentlichen in den Jahren 1909/10 fertiggestellte Gebäude erinnert an einen großartigen barocken Schloßbau. Es ist ein eindrucksvolles Beispiel für die Entwicklung der deutschen Architektur zum Beginn des 20. Jahrhunderts. Genau diesen Baustil hatte Paul Schultze-Naumburg mit seinen «Kulturarbeiten» angeregt. So nimmt es auch nicht wunder, daß im Heft Nr. 1 der «Dresdner Künstlerhefte» 1909 die Badehausneubauten in Bad Elster eine große Rolle spielten. Der plastische Schmuck an und in der Alberthalle stammt vom Bildhauer Karl Gross-Dresden. Ihm haben wir diesen prächtigen Palast des Wassermannes zu verdanken. Der Brückenübergang über den Elstertunnel mit den großen Blumenfischen und der Schmuck in der etwas zurückhaltenderen aber nicht weniger schönen nördlichen Treppenhalle sind Werke des Bildhauers Ulrich aus Dresden. Er hat auch die Luxuszelle, die sogenannte Königszelle, gestaltet. In den Jahren 1926/27 wurde der südlich gelegene Badeflügel aufgestockt. Aus dieser Zeit stammt auch die dazugehörige Eingangshalle. In ihrem dekorativen Schmuck tritt die Stilauffassung des Werkbundes deutlich zu Tage. Die Architekten Schilling & Graebener haben mit ihrem Badehausneubau Maßstäbe für die später in diesem Bereich geschaffenen Gebäude gesetzt. Ausgenommen davon ist das direkt der Alberthalle gegenüber gelegene Kurhaus. Dieses schon in den Jahren 1888/90 errichtete Gebäude ist ein Werk des Landbaumeisters Trobsch aus Zwickau. Es erinnert mit seiner leichten und filigranen Fassadengestaltung an einen italienischen Renaissance-Palast. Der Bau beinhaltete neben mehreren Fremdenzimmern und Räumlichkeiten für den Restaurant- und Casinobetrieb auch den neuen, großen und sehr prächtigen Kursaal, eine Bibliothek und verschiedene andere Gesellschaftsräume. Ganz dem Wunsch einer aus dem Jahre

In contrast to the outwardly rather reserved appearing dome-shaped hall of the forest wing, the village profile is quite impressively marked by the facade of the bath building located on Bad Street. The Albert Hall with its two side wings which were created by the architects Schilling & Graebener in cooperation with government architect Reh of the Royal Building Administration makes all other parts of the building complex take a back seat. And justly so, since the building which was mainly completed in the years 1909–10 is reminiscent of a grand Baroque castle structure. It is an impressive example for the development of German architecture from the beginning of the 20th century. It is exactly this style of building which Paul Schultze-Naumburg inspired with his «cultural works». Therefore, it is not surprising that in issue number one of the «Dresdner Kuenstlerhefte» (Dresden Artistic Magazines) in 1909 the new buildings of the bath house in Bad Elster played a major role. The plastique ornamentation in and on the Albert Hall were created by sculptor Karl Gross from Dresden. To him we owe this splendid palace of Aquarius. The bridge overpass over the Elster tunnel with the large floral fish and the decoration in a somewhat less striking but nonetheless beautiful northern staircase hall are works by the sculptor Ulrich from Dresden. He also designed the luxurious cabana, the so-called Royal Cabana. Only in the years 1926–27 was the southern bath wing extended. Also the entrance hall which belongs to this building dates back to that time. Its ornate decoration clearly represents the stylistic ideas of the builders of the period. The architects Schiller & Graebener had with their new building of the bath house set a standard for the buildings to be created in this area subsequently. An exception is the spa house which is located directly opposite Albert Hall. This structure which was already erected in the years 1888–90 was a work of the country builder Trobsch from Zwickau. The light and filigree design of its facade is reminiscent of an Italian Renaissance palace. The building accommodated, apart from several guest rooms and facilities for restaurant and casino operation, also the new grand and very splendid spa hall, a library and various other rooms for social functions. In accordance with a request expressed in a petition from 1874, the spa house became the social center of town. The predecessor building of a «Cursaal» (spa hall) which had been erected approxima-

1874 stammenden Petition entsprechend, wurde das Kurhaus zum gesellschaftlichen Zentrum des Ortes. Der etwa in der Mitte der sechziger Jahre des vorigen Jahrhunderts neben dem damaligen «Hotel de Saxe» errichtete Vorgängerbau eines «Cursaales» diente vordergründig als Speisesaal. Deshalb wurde im Sommer 1874 besagte Petition verfaßt. In diesem mit 111 Unterschriften maßgeblicher Persönlichkeiten versehenen Brief wurde sehr höflich, aber auch nachdrucksvoll auf den bestehenden Mangel hingewiesen. Zu den Unterzeichnern gehörten Clara von Bülow, Baron Franz von Hahn-Kurland, Consul Scharf aus Tahiti, Fürst Barclay de Tolly-Weymarn, Pierre de Kapnist-Chambellan de S. M. L'Empereur de Russie und auch der Graf von Schulenburg-Hohenberg. Es dürfte kaum ein anderes Gebäude in Bad Elster mit so weitreichender Unterstützung geben.

Im Ort selbst wird wohl keiner die Fertigstellung des neuen Kurhauses so herbeigesehnt haben, wie der königlich sächsische Musikdirektor Christoph Wolfgang Hilf (1818–1911). Er, der von Felix Mendelssohn Bartholdy, Robert Schumann und Franz Liszt gepriesene Geigenvirtuose, hatte im Jahre 1851 die Badekapelle von seinem Vater Johann Christoph Hilf übernommen. Gemeinsam mit seinem Bruder Christian Adam Arno Hilf und dem Vater, der noch 1883 (als Hundertjähriger) dem Ensemble angehörte, war er das musische Juwel des Bades. Den verlockenden Erfolg von Konzertreisen hintenanstellend, widmete er sich vorwiegend den Aufgaben in seinem Heimatort. Bad Elster war und ist für seine niveauvolle Kurmusik bekannt, letztendlich ein Verdienst der Familie Hilf. Ch. W. Hilf, der weit über die Grenzen des Vogtlandes hinaus bekannte Musiker, hatte im Gewandhausorchester in Leipzig gespielt. Der neue Konzertsaal wird für ihn ein Traum gewesen sein.

Als das Kurhaus 1890 mit seinem «Festgesang für gemischten Chor und Orchester» eingeweiht wurde, hatte er die Badekapelle zu einem beachtenswerten Klangkörper entwickelt. Mit Sicherheit gab das Orchester auch Konzerte im Palast-Hotel «Wettiner Hof», vermutlich aber vorwiegend in dem Vorgängerbau des heute leider verwaisten Gebäudes. Nach einem Brand wurde das Hotel in den Jahren 1907/08 von den Chemnitzer Architekten Zapp & Basarke in neuer Gestalt aufgebaut. Der prachtvolle Jugendstilbau bildete mit seinen Sälen und zahlreichen Salons den festlichen Rahmen für viele erstrangige Ereignisse in Bad Elster, die auch dazu beitrugen, eine immer größer werdende Zahl wohlhabender Kurgäste in den Badeort zu ziehen. Neben dem sächsischen König dürfte wohl der russische Ministerpräsident Stolpin der hochrangigste Gast des Hauses gewesen sein. Die Sicherheitsvorkehrungen waren bei seinem Besuch im Juni 1911 so groß, daß nicht einmal der ortsansässige Briefträger das Gebäude betreten durfte. Die für den Ort überhöht erscheinende Absicherung wurde zunächst belächelt, als Stolpin aber am 19. September 1911 nach einem Attentat starb, trauerte der ganze Badeort. Man hatte einen geschätzten Kurgast verloren, denn der Herr Ministerpräsident beabsichtigte auch 1912 wieder nach Bad Elster zu kommen. Bad Elster war zu einem Weltbad geworden.

Die Ansprüche an das gesamte Badeleben, insbesondere an die gesellschaftliche Umrahmung, stiegen ständig. Deshalb, und auch aus Prestigegründen, wurde die Errichtung eines neuen Theaters ins Auge gefaßt. Mit staatlicher Billigung wurde 1912 eine Gesellschaft, die sogenannte Theater-GmbH, gegründet. In einem Zeitungsartikel vom 11. Januar 1913 ist zu lesen: «Mit Unterstützung der Kgl. Staatsregierung hat sich eine GmbH mit recht beträchtlichen Mitteln und noch wesentlich höherem Hinterhalt zusammengetan, um ein zeitgemäßes Theater in günstiger Lage zu schaffen, das sich schon rein äußerlich den Monumentalbauten in nächster Umgebung des Badeplatzes anschließen soll.» Die Entscheidung war gefallen. An Stelle des «Hotel de Saxe» und des dazugehörigen «Cursaales» sollte ein modernes Theater in Verbindung mit einem Hotelneubau entstehen. Der ebenfalls von den Architekten Zapp & Basarke geschaffene Ge-

tely in the middle of the 1860's next to the former «Hotel de Saxe» was mainly used as a dining hall. In the letter which was signed by 111 influential people this lack was pointed out in a polite but emphatic manner. Among the undersigned were Clara von Buelow, Baron Franz von Hahn-Kurland, Council Scharf from Tahiti, Prince Barclay de Tolly-Weymarn, Pierre de Kapnist-Chambellan de S.M. L'Empereur de Russie and also the Count of Schulenburg-Hohenberg. Probably no other building in Bad Elster received such far-reaching support. In the town itself there was probably no one who so longed for the completion of the spa house as did the royal Saxonian musical director Christoph Wolfgang Hilf. He, the violin virtuoso who had been praised by Felix Mendelssohn, Robert Schumann and Franz Liszt, had taken over the spa band from his father Johann Christian Hilf in 1851. Forgoing the enticing success of concert tours, he primarily dedicated himself to the tasks of his home town. Bad Elster was and is known for the high level of its spa music which in the final analysis is the merit of the Hilf family. Ch. W. Hilf (1818–1911), who was well known far beyond the borders of the Vogtland, had played in the Gewandhaus orchestra in Leipzig. When the spa house was inaugurated in 1890 with a «festive song for mixed choir and orchestra», he had developed the spa band into a remarkable musical body. The orchestra surely also gave concerts in the palace hotel Wettiner Hof, probably however predominantly in the predecessor building of the structure which today is unfortunately deserted. Since after a fire the hotel was reerected in new form in 1907-08 by the Chemnitz architects Zapp & Basarke. The splendid art nouveau building formed with its halls and numerous salons the festive framework for many first-ranking events in Bad Elster which contributed to attracting an ever increasing number of affluent spa guests to the health resort. Next to the Saxon king, the Russian Minister-President Stolpin was probably the highest ranking guest of the house. During his visit in June of 1911, security measures were so extensive that not even the local postman was allowed to enter the building. This security consciousness which seemed for the town to be exaggerated was at first smiled upon, but when Stolpin died on September 19, 1911 due to an assassination, the entire bath town mourned him. They had lost an appreciated spa guest since the Minister-President had intended to return to Bad Elster in 1912. Bad Elster had become a world bath.

The demands on the entire bath life, especially on the social framework, were constantly increasing. Therefore, as well as for reasons of prestige, the establishment of a new theater was planned. A newspaper article dated January 11, 1913 reads as follows: «With the

König Friedrich August III. (3. v. l.) mit Kurdirektor von Alberti (5. v. l.) und Begleitung nach der traditionellen Auerhahnjagd 1917 in Bad Elster.

King Friedrich August III (third from left) with spa director von Alberti (fifth from left) and company after the traditionel capercaillie hunt in Bad Elster in 1917.

17

bäudekomplex entstand innerhalb eines Jahres für eine Bausumme von 1,3 Mio. Mark. Am 22. Mai 1914 erfolgte im Beisein des sächsischen Königs die feierliche Einweihung des Theaters. Zur Eröffnung wurde das vom Apotheker Carl Klingener verfaßte Festspiel «Quellenzauber» aufgeführt. Bis heute hat der imposante Gebäudekomplex nichts von seiner monumentalen Wirkung verloren. Er ist wesentlicher Bestandteil eines eindrucksvollen städtebaulichen Ensembles. Die in den nächsten Jahren anstehenden Restaurierungsarbeiten werden ihm alten, neuen Glanz verleihen.

Ende der zwanziger Jahre setzt eine neuerliche Bauphase ein. Das wohl eindruckvollste Gebäude aus dieser Zeit ist die im Bauhausstil errichtete Wandelhalle mit Salz- und Moritzquelle. Dieses in den Jahren 1928/29 errichtete Gebäude ist das Werk des Ministerialrates Dr. Kramer und des Regierungsbaurates Dutzmann. Beide Architekten gehörten zur Sächsischen Hochbau-Direktion. Sie waren unermüdlich für und in Bad Elster tätig. So ist ihnen auch die völlige Neugestaltung des Badeplatzes zuzuschreiben. Das schlichte aber zweckmäßige Ensemble entstand in den Jahren 1933/34. Die etwas hinter den Bäumen versteckte Dreiquellenhalle bildet mit ihrer Laterne und der darauf befindlichen goldenen Brunnenfigur den gestalterischen Höhepunkt des nach Süden geöffneten Platzes.

Die Figur scheint in ihrem Krug den Born des heilsamen Schatzes der Minerale zu tragen. Beim Betreten der Halle kann man sich in die Zauberwelt der Kristalle und der Quellnymphen versetzt fühlen. Leider wurde das Thema bei der inneren Umgestaltung der Quellenhalle in den fünfziger Jahren nur teilweise aufgenommen bzw. dem Zeitgeschmack entsprechend verfremdet.

Noch bevor die Architekten Kramer und Dutzmann mit der Gestaltung des Badeplatzes begannen, hatten sie das Kurhaus im Inneren völlig umgestaltet. Fast möchte man diesen Gestaltwandel bedauern, vor allem wenn man Bilder vom alten repräsentativen Saal gesehen hat. Beim Besichtigen der im April 1933 fertiggestellten Räume wird aber eine klare in sich geschlossene künstlerische Gestaltung erkennbar, die der Gesamtwirkung des Gebäudes nicht unbedingt entgegensteht. Bei der in naher Zukunft einsetzenden regen Bautätigkeit in Bad Elster wird gerade diese Stilverträglichkeit ein Maßstab sein, denn die historische Substanz bildet zusammen mit den Kurparkanlagen den unverwechselbaren Kern der kleinen Kurstadt im oberen Vogtland.

Die Parkanlagen

Der Kurpark ist ein grünes Bindeglied im Herzen des Ortes. In ihm und um ihn herum hat sich Bad Elster entwickelt, ist es in der ersten Hälfte unseres Jahrhunderts zu einem Weltbad geworden. Die in den Talbereichen der Weißen Elster und des Bärenlohbaches befindlichen Anlagen leiten an ihren Endpunkten in die umgebende Landschaft über. Sie sind über 140 Jahre gewachsen und heute unter Denkmalschutz gestellt. Von Kurgästen, Touristen und Einwohnern werden die Kurparkanlagen wegen ihrer Ruhe, dem wertvollen Baumbestand, den weitläufigen Rhododendronpflanzungen und den vielseitigen Blumenbeeten sehr geschätzt. Die mit der Pflege der Anlagen betrauten Gärtner sind von alters her Meister ihres Faches. Ebenso wie bei den Bauwerken waren Fachkompetenz und ein starkes Ein-

support of the royal state government a corporation with quite considerable means and even more considerable reserves has been formed in order to create a contemporary theater in a favorable location which is intended to be appropriate already from the viewpoint of outward appearance to the monumental buildings in the proximity of the bath site.» The decision was made. At the site of the «Hotel de Saxe» and the «Cursaal» belonging to it, a modern theater was to be created in connection with a new hotel structure. This building complex, which was as well designed by the architects Zapp & Basarke, was erected within a year at the cost of 1.3 million Deutsch Marks. On May 22, 1914 the festive inauguration of the theater took place in the presence of the king of Saxony. At the opening festive play «Quellenzauber» (Spring Charm) by the pharmacist Carl Klinger was performed.

Even to the present day the imposing building complex has lost none of its monumental impressiveness. The restorative works which will be conducted in the next few years will provide it with old/new splendor.

At the end of the 20's a new building phase was begun. Probably the most impressive building from this period is the pump hall erected in the Bauhaus style with Salt and Moritz Spring. This building, which was erected in 1928–29, is the work of principal Dr. Kramer and government architect Dutzmann. Both architects belonged to the Saxonian building construction administration. Also, the entire new design of the bath site is their work. The simple but functional ensemble was established in 1933-34. The three-spring hall, which is today somewhat hidden behind trees, forms with its lantern and its golden fountain statue the architectural highlights of the square which is open to the south.

When entering the Albert Bath one feels transposed into the empire of Aquarius, into the magical world of crystals and spring nymphs. The fountain figure seems to carry in its mug the fount of the wholesome treasure of minerals towards he who enters. Unfortunately the theme was only partly carried on or changed according to the prevailing taste when the interior of the spring hall was redesigned in the 50's.

Before the architects Kramer and Dutzmann began designing the bath site, they had completely redesigned the interior of the spa. One is almost tempted to regret this change, especially after having seen pictures of the old representative hall. When visiting the rooms completed in April, 1933 a clear uniform artistic design becomes, however, obvious which does not form any contrast to the overall impression of the building. The building activities which will soon be begun in Bad Elster will be measured in terms of compatibility of style since the historical substance forms together with the spa park facilities the unmistakable core of the small health resort in Upper Vogtland.

The Park Facilities

The spa park is a green bond in the heart of town. Bad Elster has developed in and around it. The finishing points of these facilities situated in the valley areas of the Weisse Elster River and the Baerenloh Brook provide a transition into the surroundings. They have grown over more than 140 years and have today been declared a national monument. Spa guests, tourists and residents highly appreciate the spa park facilities because of their quiet, the valuable old trees, the far-reaching rhododendron plantations and the variety of flower beds. The gardeners in charge of cultivating the park have always been masters in their field. As with the buildings, expert competence and a strong sensitivity for the regional features were basic prerequisites for employment in the spa park.

Der «Louisa-See», heute Gondelteich, im Kurpark um 1900.

The Louisa Lake, today gondolla pond, in the spa park around 1900.

Salzquelle mit Wandelbahn um 1900, davor Blumenbeete und Hygiea-Gruppe.

Salt spring with walking area around 1900. In front, flower beds and Hygiea group.

fühlungsvermögen in die territorialen Gegebenheiten Grundvoraussetzungen, um eine Anstellung im Kurpark zu erhalten.

Nach Übernahme des Bades 1849 war man sich in der Residenzstadt Dresden darüber im klaren, daß das Staatsbad einen Kurpark braucht. Deshalb wollte man den Hofgärtner Terscheck auch sofort mit der Gestaltung der Anlagen betrauen. Das Vorhaben scheiterte jedoch an dessen Alter und Gesundheitszustand. So nahm man schon 1851 zu keinem Geringeren als dem Weimarer Hofgärtner Eduard Petzold, Schüler des Fürsten Pückler in Muskau, Verbindung auf. Für die Anlage eines Parkes im Bärenloher Tal sollten die 1852 von den Ständen der vogtländischen Kreise gestifteten 6000 Taler verwendet werden. Dafür waren zunächst aber umfangreiche Grundstückskäufe erforderlich; so verzögerte sich das Vorhaben. Erst im Jahre 1855 wurde entschieden, daß die Anlage nach dem Petzold'schen Plan auszuführen sei. Im selben Jahr lieferte Petzold noch einen zweiten Plan für die zur Badedirektion gehörenden Flächen im Elstertal. Man hatte aber vermutlich schon zuvor festgestellt, daß aus der Ferne ein Gartenkünstler dem Bade nur wenig dienlich sein kann. Deshalb wurde der aus Hof stammende Kunstgärtner Friedrich Prohaska im Februar 1853 als erster Badegärtner in Elster angestellt. Auch er legte Pläne zur Gestaltung und Erweiterung von Anlagen vor. Offenbar war man mit seinen Projekten zufrieden, denn er erhielt für seine Bemühungen um den Kurpark die Goldene Medaille vom Albrechtsorden. Bis zu seinem Tode 1875 hatte er maßgeblichen Anteil an der Entwicklung der Gartenanlagen und damit am Wohlbefinden der Kurgäste in Bad Elster.

Leider können wir heute weder die Petzoldschen noch die Prohaskaschen Anlagen im Kurpark erkennen. Durch den wechselnden Zeitgeschmack und die ständigen Erweiterungen wurden die Parkanlagen des öfteren verändert.

Das traf auch auf das Werk von Prohaskas Nachfolger Carl Große zu. Eine Ausnahme bildet der Rosengarten. Auf dem Gelände des heutigen Rosengartens hatten bis 1882 die Scheune und der Kuhstall des Rittergutes gestanden. Nach deren Abriß unterbreitete der damalige Badedirektor Otho den Vorschlag, die entstandene Platzfläche in eine französische Gartenanlage umzuwandeln. Zu diesem Zwecke wurden in Bad Elster mehrere Pläne angefertigt, die in Dresden aber offensichtlich keine rechte Zustimmung fanden. Was durchaus verständlich ist, denn bei den Gartenkünstlern der zweiten Hälfte des 19. Jahrhunderts war der französische Geschmack verpönt, es herrschte die landschaftliche Gartengestaltung vor. Deshalb wollte man zunächst auch prüfen lassen, ob nicht eine «Parkanlage» auf der besagten Fläche günstiger wäre. Der Staatsminister von Nostiz-Wallwitz ließ sich zu diesem Zweck Pläne des königlichen Gartendirektors Bouché vorlegen. Allerdings hatte man in Bad Elster nicht auf seine Entscheidung gewartet und schon mit den Ausführungsarbeiten nach eigenen Plänen begonnen. Die daraus resultierende Verstim-

After taking over the bath in 1849 it was clear to the officials in the royal residence town of Dresden that a state bath needs a spa park. Therefore it was intended to make the court gardener Terscheck immediately responsible for the design of the facilities. This plan was however thwarted by his age and state of health. Therefore, already in 1851 no lesser man was contacted than the Weimar court gardener Eduard Petzold, disciple of Prince Pueckler in Muskau. For the establishment of a park in the Baerenloh Valley the 6,000 Taler donated by the estates of the Vogtland districts in 1852 were supposed to be used. But at first, comprehensive purchases of real estate were required; thus the project was delayed. Only in 1855 was it decided to design the facility according to Petzold's plan. In the same year Petzold provided a second plan for the areas in the Elster Valley which belonged to the bath administration. It had however probably been discovered already earlier that a distant garden architect was of little help to the bath. Therefore the artistic gardener Friedrich Prohaska from Hof was employed in February of 1853 as first bath gardener in Elster. He also submitted plans for the design and extension of the facilities. His projects were obviously satisfying because he received for his efforts about the spa park the golden medal of the Albrecht order. Up to his death in 1875 he was of considerable importance for the development of the garden facilities and thus for the well-being of the spa guests in Bad Elster.

Unfortunately today we can recognize neither Petzold's nor Prohaska's designs in the spa park. Due to the change in prevailing taste and continuous expansions, the park facilities were repeatedly modified.

This was also true for the work of Prohaska's successor Carl Grosse. An exception is the rose garden. Up to 1882 the barn and the cow shed of the knight's estate had been located on the area of today's rose garden. After their demolition, the then bath director Otho submitted his proposal to turn this area into a French garden facility. For this purpose several plans were drawn up in Bad Elster which, however, obviously did not win approval in Dresden. This is quite plausible since the garden architects of the second half of the 19th century looked down upon French taste. A landscape garden design prevailed at the time. Therefore it was intended to first find out whether a park facility in the previously mentioned area might meet with more favor. The state minister von Nostiz-Wallwitz had the royal garden director Bouché submit plans for this purpose. In Bad Elster, however, they had not waited for his decision, but began the works according to plans of their own. Fortunately the resulting disgruntlement could be resolved on site by making slight modifications in the facility under construction. Of course Bouché had not planned the rose garden which we see today. The regular structure of paths is, however, still quite obvious. But outside the actual spa park even today we often encounter the work of Prohaska and Grosse. Both had laid the basis

mung konnte glücklicherweise vor Ort durch geringfügige Veränderungen an der in Ausführung befindlichen Anlage beseitigt werden. Natürlich hatte Bouché nicht den Rosengarten geplant, den wir heute vorfinden. Die regelmäßige Wegestruktur können wir aber noch sehr deutlich ablesen. Außerhalb des eigentlichen Kurparks treffen wir allerdings noch des öfteren auf das Werk Prohaskas und Großes. Beide haben den Grundstock für das umfangreiche Wanderwegenetz am Brunnenberg und in der weiteren Umgebung des Bades gelegt. Schon im Oktober 1877 hatte das Wegenetz eine Gesamtlänge von 9562 m. Noch erstaunlicher ist aber, daß im besagten Wegeaufmaß schon eine Vielzahl von Schutzhütten verzeichnet war. Zu ihnen gehörten die Eremitage, das Waldhaus und auch die Kreuzkapelle. Nicht selten lesen Kurgäste mit ungläubigem Blick die an den Hütten angebrachten Jahreszahlen. Natürlich wurden die Hütten zum Teil ausgebessert und erneuert, ihr Ansehen hat sich dabei aber nur unwesentlich verändert. In Bad Elster ist man sehr stolz auf diesen kostbaren Schatz aus dem vergangenen Jahrhundert. Die Blockhütten zeugen von einer bodenständigen Handwerkskunst. Mit ihren Verzierungen wirken sie geradezu festlich im Vergleich zu den heutigen Modellen.

Als nach dem Bau des neuen Kurhauses im September 1890 die Gestaltung der Außenanlagen in diesem Bereich nach einem Plan des Dresdner Gartenbaudirektors Max Bertram begann, eröffneten sich neue Perspektiven für den Kurpark. Die Oberaufsicht führte der Königliche Gartendirektor Bouché. Aber nicht sein neuerliches Wirken in Bad Elster sollte von weitreichender Bedeutung sein, sondern das des erst 23jährigen Paul Schindel. Man kann es als eine Sternstunde für den Ort ansehen, daß ihm die Bauleitung von Max Bertram übertragen wurde. Zu diesem Zeitpunkt hat er es sich wohl nicht träumen lassen, daß er später einmal das Gesicht des ganzen Ortes verändern würde.

Schon am 1. April 1892 wurde Paul Schindel auf Anraten von Bouché und Bertram als Badgärtner eingestellt. Voller Ideenreichtum begann er mit der Umgestaltung der Anlagen. Auf den Gartenbauausstellungen in Dresden und Berlin hatte er schon Preise für seine Entwürfe bekommen. In Leipzig zur Internationalen Jubiläums-Gartenbauausstellung 1893 wurden seine Pläne für die Kurparkanlagen in Bad Elster mit der Goldenen Medaille gewürdigt. In den Folgejahren arbeitete er unermüdlich an der Um- und Neugestaltung des Kurparkes. Bad Elster verdankt ihm den König-Albert-Park, den Kurpark, den Südpark mit dem Gondelteich (früher Louisa-See) und dem Rosengarten, das Licht-, Luft- und Schwimmbad, den Nordpark mit den Tennisplätzen, die Windschutzstreifen, die Rodelbahn, die Kegelbahn, einen Teil der Schutzhütten, die Anlagen an der Waldquelle und das Naturtheater. Ebenso lag die Erschließung der Moorgründe in seiner Hand. Alle Arbeiten wurden so eingerichtet, daß sie zur Verschönerung des Ortes beitrugen. Fast als Nebenprodukt verdankt ihm das Staatsbad ein großes Brauchwasserreservoir. Paul Schindel wurde durch seine Tätigkeit weit über die Grenzen Bad Elsters hinaus bekannt. 1912 wurde er für seinen unermüdlichen Einsatz mit dem Albrechtskreuz geehrt. 1924, drei Jahre nach seinem Tod, wurde ihm zu Ehren eine Eiche im König-Albert-Park gepflanzt.

Schindels Nachfolger war Max Haschke. In die Zeit seiner Tätigkeit sollten wesentliche Veränderungen und Erweiterungen der Kurparkanlagen fallen. Dabei stand ihm der Stadtgartendirektor Dresdens, von Uslar, zur Seite. Er war schon 1919 nach Bad Elster beordert worden. In der Folge war von Uslar des öfteren beratend im Kurpark tätig, zumindest ist dies bis 1924 belegt.

Mit dem Gestaltungsauftrag für das Elsterstadion an Prof. Gustav Allinger wurde die gartenkünstlerische Kontinuität gewahrt. Das in den Jahren 1925 bis 1931 angelegte Stadion ist eine gelungene Erweiterung des Südparkes.

Gustav Allinger erhielt auch den Auftrag für die Umgestaltung der

Das Kurhaus nach Fertigstellung der neuen Außenanlagen 1891.
The spa house after completion of the new outside facilities in 1891.

for a comprehensive network of hiking paths on the Brunnenberg Mountain and in the more distant reaches of the path. Already in October 1877 the network of paths totaled 9,562 meters (31,370 feet). It is even more amazing that in the mentioned record of paths, already a number of refuges was listed, including the Erimitage (hermitage), the Waldhaus (forest house) and the Kreuzkapelle (cross chapel). Not infrequently are spa guests amazed when reading the dates on the shelters. The refuges have of course been partly repaired and restored, but their outward appearance has hardly changed. The people of Bad Elster are very proud of this precious treasure from the last century. The log cabins testify to indigenous handicraft. With their decoration they appear almost festive compared to today's models.

When after the erection of the new spa house in September 1890, the design of the outside facilities in this area was begun according to a plan of the Dresden garden architect Max Bertram, new perspectives opened for the spa park. The royal garden director Bouché supervised the work. But not his renewed efforts in Bad Elster should be of far reaching importance, but rather that of the only 23 year old Paul Schindel. It may be regarded as a historic moment for the town that Max Bertram made him responsible for the construction management. At that moment he probably could not imagine in his dreams of changing the face of the entire town at a later date. Upon recommendation of Bouché and Bertram, Paul Schindel was hired as bath gardener already on April 1, 1892. Filled with ideas, he began redesigning the facilities. He had previously received awards for his drafts at the exhibitions for garden architecture in Dresden and Berlin. During the international jubilee exhibition of garden architecture in Leipzig in 1893 he was awarded a gold medal for his plans for the spa park facilities in Bad Elster. In subsequent years he untiringly occupied himself with the redesign and the new design of the spa park. Bad Elster owes to him the King Albert park; the spa park; the south park with the gondola pond (formerly Luisa Lake) and the rose garden; the light, air and swimming pool; north park with tennis courts; the wind-sheltered zone; the toboggan slide; the bowling alley; some of the refuges; the facilities at the forest spring and the nature theater. Also the development of the swamps laid in his hands. All works were designed in such a way that they contributed to the enhancement of the town. Almost as a side product, the state bath owes a large water reservoir for fire emergencies to him.

Due to his activities, Paul Schindel became famous far beyond the borders of Bad Elster. In 1924, three years after his death, an oak tree was planted in his honor in King Albert park which is called the Schindel Oak. By now it has grown into an imposing tree.

Schindel's successor was Max Haschke. The period of his activities was marked by considerable changes and extensions of the spa park facilities. He was assisted by the municipal garden director of Dres-

Moritzquelle mit Wandelbahn und Hygiea-Gruppe um 1900.
Moritz Spring with walking area and Hygiea group, around 1900.

Cafe «Waldquelle» um 1900 am schattigen Bahnhofsweg.
«Waldquelle» (forest spring) coffee house, around 1900, on the shaded railway path.

Parkanlage an der neuen Wandelhalle. In den Jahren 1933/34 übernahm dann der Direktor der Staatlichen Gartenanlagen Sachsens, Hermann Schüttauf, die gärtnerische Gestaltung des neuen Badeplatzes. Eine bis in unsere Zeit erhaltene, repräsentative Anlage, die sowohl mit den Gebäuden als auch mit der umgebenden Landschaft im Einklang steht. Die Handschrift Schüttaufs ist noch an vielen anderen Stellen des Kurparks ablesbar. Das Springbrunnenbeet hinter der Wandelhalle und die Umgebung des Musikpavillons am Kurhaus sind die eindruckvollsten Beispiele.

Glücklicherweise ist Bad Elster im Zweiten Weltkrieg von Kampfhandlungen verschont geblieben, so daß der einzigartige Kurpark ohne Schaden über die Zeit kam.

Großes Verdienst für die Erhaltung der Gesamtanlage erwarb sich nach 1945 Otto Bernhard. Mit sachgerechter Pflege und der Pflanzung unzähliger Rhododendren machte er den Kurpark noch attraktiver. Eine für die Kuranlagen sehr wesentliche Veränderung, die in seine Dienstzeit fällt, ist besonders herauszuheben. Gemeinsam mit Hermann Schüttauf hat er der Anlage hinter der Wandelhalle ein neues Gesicht gegeben. Schon 1950 war hier nach Plänen Schüttaufs ein neuer Springbrunnen entstanden. Später wurde dann der dahinter liegende Wald aufgelichtet und so eine Sichtbeziehung zum Brunnenberg hergestellt. 1966 konnte die von Bildhauer Hempel in Dresden geschaffene Brunnenschale aufgestellt werden. Der heutige Kurpark wird von einer Vielzahl in der zweiten Hälfte des vergangenen Jahrhunderts und um die Jahrhundertwende gepflanzter Bäume geprägt. Da finden sich stattliche Eichen, Buchen und Ulmen. Neben den Fichten an den Hanglagen beherrschen die Erlen vor allem das Bild der Talbereiche. Zu ihnen gesellen sich herrliche Lärchen, Douglasien, Weymoutskiefern und Tannen. Besonderheiten in den Kurparkanlagen von Bad Elster sind der Tulpenbaum, die Schindeleiche, zwei ungewöhnliche Eschen und die eichenblättrigen Hainbuchen am Badeplatz. Jeder Gast kann in dem fast 50 ha großen Areal etwas für seinen Geschmack finden. Da sind die repräsentativen breiten Promenadenwege mit ihren weißen Bänken ebenso vertreten wie die behaglichen zurückgezogenen Ruheplätze. Besonders erfrischend ist der an der Weißen Elster entlang führende Dammweg. Der Fluß ist in diesem Bereich kaskadenartig ausgebaut und wirkt somit besonders belebend. Für weitläufigere Spaziergänge wird ein gut ausgebautes Wegenetz in die den Ort umschließenden Waldungen angeboten. An ihnen befinden sich gepflegte Bankplätze, Schutzhütten, Restaurants und Cafes. Im Frühling stehen die Anlagen im Blütenflor der Traubenkirschen. Diese werden durch die in allen Bereichen dominierenden Rhododendren abgelöst. Die günstigen Klima- und Standortbedingungen haben diese Pflanzen zu prachtvollen Blütenwänden heranwachsen lassen. In den Monaten Mai und Juni ist Bad Elster ein Eldorado für Rhododendronfreunde. Schon zur Zeit der Rhododendronblüte werden die zentralen Kurbereiche durch die Pracht tausen-

den von Uslar. He had been ordered to Bad Elster already in 1919. In the subsequent period von Uslar repeatedly acted as a consultant in the spa park, a fact which is at least documented until 1924.

When the design assignment for the Elster stadium was given to Professor Gustav Allinger, the garden architectural continuity was preserved. The stadium which was constructed from 1925 to 1931 is a successful extension of the south park. Gustav Allinger also received the assignment for the redesign of the park facilities at the new pump hall. In the years 1933-34 the director of the state gardens of Saxony Hermann Schuettauf was responsible for the garden design of the new bath site. It is a representative facility which has been preserved up to our time and is in tune with both the buildings and the surrounding countryside. Schuettauf's imprint is still obvious in many other parts of the spa park. The fountain bed behind the pump hall and the area surrounding the music pavilion at the spa house are impressive examples.

Fortunately Bad Elster was spared combat in World War II so that the unique spa park survived undamaged.

After 1945 Otto Bernhard achieved great merit for the maintenance of the overall facility. With expert cultivation and the planting of numerous rhododendrons he made the spa park even more attractive. One change which is very essential for the spa facilities and which took place during his term of office deserves particular emphasis. Together with Hermann Schuettauf, he has given a new face to the facility behind the pump hall. Already in 1950 a new fountain was erected here according to Schuettauf's plans. Later the forest beyond was thinned and thus a visual connection to the Brunnenberg Mountain was established. In 1966 the fountain bowl created by the sculptor Hempel in Dresden was erected.

Today's spa park is marked by a great number of trees planted in the second half of the last century and at the turn of the century. There are stately oaks, beeches and elms. Apart from the fir trees on the slopes, yew trees dominate the picture, especially in the valley areas. They are accompanied by beautiful larches, Douglas firs, Weymouth pines and evergreens. Specialties in the spa park facilities of Bad Elster are the Tulip Tree, the Schindel Oak, two unusual ash trees and the oak-leafed hornbeams at the bath site. Every guest can find something to his liking in the almost 50 hectare (124 acre) large area. There are the representative broad promenades with the white benches as well as the comfortable withdrawn resting areas. The dam path leading along the Weisse Elster River is particularly refreshing. The river has in that area been extended in a cascade-like manner and thus appears particularly revitalizing. For farther reaching hikes, a well-maintained network of paths in the forests surrounding the town is offered. Along them are cultivated benches, refuges, restaurants and coffee shops. In spring the facilities are graced with blooming bird cherries. They are followed by the rhododendrons dominating in all areas. The

der Frühjahrsblumen hervorgehoben. Sie konkurrieren oft mit den herrlichsten Blumenwiesen.

Einen besonderen Schmuckwert erhalten die 1150 m² umfassenden Beetflächen im Sommerblumenflor. Paul Schindel war es, der die Teppichgärtnerei in Bad Elster weithin bekannt gemacht hat. Heute finden wir vor allem die farbenprächtigen Mischpflanzungen vor, wie sie von Schüttauf in den Dreißigerjahren gestaltet wurden. Es wird zu diesem Zweck in der Gärtnerei des Staatsbades eine Vielzahl von Arten und Sorten herangezogen. Insgesamt sind es über 55 000 Pflanzen allein im Sommer. Gärtnerischer Sachverstand und das optimale Klima lassen die Blütenpracht der Knollenbegonien in einem besonderen Glanz erscheinen. Der Sommer beginnt in Bad Elster etwas später, aber dafür umso prächtiger. Besonders an den sogenannten Hundstagen ist der Aufenthalt unter den schattigen Baumkronen oder an den plätschernden Brunnenanlagen sehr angenehm. Die fast zahmen Eichhörnchen und Buchfinken sorgen stets für Unterhaltung. Der ruhige sonnige Herbst hingegen verwandelt den Park in ein besonders warmes und weiches Bild. Die vielen verschiedenen Bäume bilden ein überaus farbenprächtiges Ensemble. Durch die nicht mehr so hoch stehende Sonne treten die einzelnen Konturen besser hervor. Jeder Laubbaum zeigt sein eigenes Gesicht. Besonders von den auf den Höhen befindlichen Aussichtspunkten eröffnet sich ein herrliches Bild.

Im Gegensatz zur Vielfarbigkeit des Herbstes bietet der Kurpark im Winter einen ruhigen in sich geschlossenen Anblick. Erst in dieser Jahreszeit, wenn der Schnee die Landschaft mit seiner weißen Pracht überschüttet, die Bäche und Teiche zugefroren sind oder sich Reif an den Bäumen gebildet hat, ist das Auge des Betrachters in der Lage, die räumliche Weite des Kurparks zu erfassen. Das filigrane Astwerk der Laubgehölze gibt Durchblicke frei, weithin leuchten die schneebedeckten Wiesenflächen. An klaren sonnigen Tagen tragen sogar die sonst so dunklen Fichten des Brunnenberges einen goldenen Schimmer.

favorable climate and location have made these plants grow into splendid walls of blossoms. In the months of May and June Bad Elster is an eldorado for the friends of rhododendrons. Already during the period of the rhododendron blossoms, the central spa areas are embellished with thousands of blooming spring flowers. They often compete with the most marvelous flower meadows. Particularly decorative is the blooming of summer flowers in the beds which comprise 1,150 square meters (12,380 square feet). It was Paul Schindel who made the carpet gardening famous beyond Bad Elster. Today we primarily encounter the colorful mixed plantations design by Schuettauf in the 30's. For this purpose a great number of species and variations is used in the horticulture of the state bath. In summer alone there are more than 55,000 plants. Gardening expertise and the optimal climate make the blossoms of the tuberous begonias appear in particular splendor. Summer starts a little later in Bad Elster, but all the more beautiful. Especially during the so-called dog days, the stay underneath the shady tree crowns or along the splashing fountains is particularly agreeable. The almost tame squirrels and chaffinches always provide entertainment. The quiet and sunny autumn on the other hand turns the park into a particularly warm and soft picture. The many various trees form an outstandingly colorful ensemble. Since the sun no longer stands that high in the sky, the individual contours are emphasized more strongly. Every deciduous tree shows its own face. From the vista points on the elevations, the spectator enjoys magnificent views.

In contrast to the many colors of fall, the spa park in winter offers a quiet, uniform picture. Only at this time of the year when the snow covers the landscape with its white splendor, when brooks and ponds are frozen and frost forms on the trees is the spectator able to realize the vastness of the spa park. The filigree branches of the deciduous trees offer unhampered views, the snow-covered meadows shine from the distance. On clear and sunny days even the otherwise dark fir trees of the Brunnenberg Mountain carry a golden sheen.

Terrainkurwege um Bad Elster

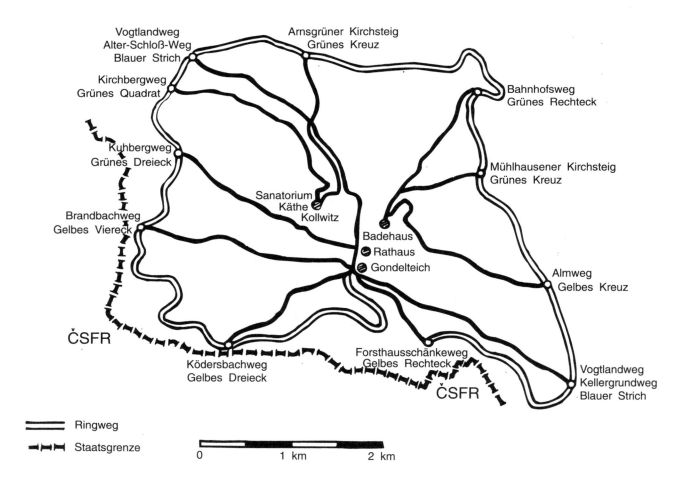

Wanderwege

In Berichten und Schriften über Bad Elster wird immer wieder die natürliche Umgebung mit ihren landschaftlichen Schönheiten besonders hervorgehoben. 1669 gab Leisner in seinem kleinen Büchlein über den Elsteraner Sauerbrunnen eine eindrucksvolle Schilderung eines Spazierganges von Adorf nach Elster: «Von daraus kan mann in den Grunde uff Wiesen/biß an den Brunn/fast stets an der Elster hinauff spatzieren. Uff beyden Seiten ist dieses Thal mit lustigen Hügeln/theils mit Getraidig angebauet/theils mit Gehöltze gezieret/daß es lustig zu sehen/bevoraus/wenn zu der Zeit im Sommer/do der Sauerling gebrauchet wird/eine Heerde Viehe von Schafen und Rindern der andern nach Weidet/und die Hirten und Schäfer ihre Schalmeyen und Hirten-Lieder hören lassen.»

Fast 200 Jahre später, als die alte Poststraße Adorf-Elster-Asch-Eger noch befahren wurde, kam 1847 als erster Brunnenarzt Dr. Robert Flechsig nach Elster. Er kam aus Oelnitz (Erzgebirge) und erkannte recht bald den Wert der obervogtländischen Landschaft für das entstehende Königlich-Sächsische Staatsbad Elster. Begeistert schreibt er über Elster: »Die Badeanstalt mit den Quellen breitet sich in einem höchst anmutigen Tale aus und ist rings von beträchtlichen mit Nadelholz besetzten Höhen umgeben, von denen sich ein lohnender, das Herz erfreuender Blick in die Nähe und Ferne ergibt.»

Um die orographischen Verhältnisse exakt erfassen zu können, ließ er für die wichtigsten Geländepunkte barometrische Höhenmessungen durchführen. Die Angaben erfolgten in Pariser Fuß. Die Meereshöhe des Badeplatzes wurde mit 1495 Pariser Fuß ermittelt.

Ein attraktiver Kurort erhält erst sein vollkommenes Gepräge in Einheit mit der ihn umgebenden Landschaft. Er soll in seiner Gesamtheit wirken, in dem er Heil- oder Kurbehandlung mit aktiver Erholung in einer reizvollen Umgebung bei entsprechend günstigen klimatischen Verhältnissen möglich macht. Welche Bedeutung diesem Faktor während eines Kuraufenthaltes beigemessen werden muß, belegt die Tatsache, daß sich jeder Kurpatient durchschnittlich 5 1/2 Stunden täglich im Freien aufhält und zwar unabhängig von der Jahreszeit. Dabei werden ca. 12 km am Tag zu Fuß zurückgelegt und während eines 25-tägigen Kuraufenthaltes die respektable Gesamtstrecke von annähernd 300 Kilometern bewältigt. Dies stellt einen unverzichtbaren und neben der eigentlichen Behandlung auch einkalkulierten Wirkungsfaktor der Therapie dar. Kurärztliche Untersuchungen beweisen, daß sich so der Kreislauf stabilisiert und die Herzarbeit ökonomischer wird. Bei guten Kilometerleistungen geht ein hoher systolischer Blutdruck stärker zurück als in den übrigen Fällen. Auch Stoffwechselvorgänge verlaufen bei solchen Patienten günstiger, was sich an der Entwicklung des Körpergewichtes erkennen läßt.

Anregende Spaziergänge lassen sich ohne Schwierigkeit im äußeren Kurbereich durchführen. Zu diesem Zweck wurde für alle Belastungsstufen ein Wegesystem angelegt. Der Ausgangspunkt aller Wege wurde am Rande des inneren Kurbereiches gewählt. Da auf diesen Wegen nur Spaziergänge in der therapiefreien Zeit durchgeführt werden, wurde ihre Länge den örtlichen Verhältnissen entsprechend begrenzt. Auf Wanderwegen wandert man von einem Ort zum anderen, hier aber kehrt man immer wieder zum Kurort zurück. Deshalb sind sie als Terrainkurwege ausgewiesen und zusätzlich hinsichtlich ihrer Steigungsverhältnisse differenziert, um einen bestimmten Grad der Belastung auswählen und mögliche Überlastungen vermeiden zu können.

Alle Wege führen strahlenförmig nach außen bis zu einem Ringweg, der damit gleichzeitig das Ende des betreffenden Weges, also das Ziel, darstellt. Die Wegeführung wurde so vorgenommen, daß man an diesem Zielpunkt eine Einkehrstätte vorfindet, in der man eine Ruhepause einlegen kann. Zur Rückkehr in den Kurort braucht nicht der

Hiking Paths

In reports and documents about Bad Elster the natural surroundings with their beautiful countryside are repeatedly emphasized. Already in 1669 Leisner from Plauen gave in his little booklet about the Elster mineral spring an impressive description of a walk from Adorf to Elster: «From Adorf one can stroll on meadows up to the Brunn, almost always up to the Elster! On both sides this valley is adorned with nice hills, on some of which crops are growing, while others are adorned with forests. It is amusing to watch, when at the time of summer, when the mineral spring is used, herds of sheep and cattle are grazing, and the herders and shepherds can be heard playing their shawms and singing their pastoral songs.»

Almost 200 years later when the old post road Adorf- Elster-Asch-Eger was still in use, Robert Flechsig came as first spring doctor to Elster in 1847. He came from Oelsnitz (Erz Gebirge Mountains) and soon recognized the value of the countryside of the Upper Vogtland for the developing Royal Saxonian State Bath Elster. With great enthusiasm he wrote in his book about Elster: «The bath site and its springs spreads out in a very agreeable valley and is on all sides surrounded by hills on which conifers are growing and from which the spectator has a worthwhile, delightful view of near and far.»

In order to exactly record the orographic conditions he had barometric measurements of altitude performed for the most important points of the area. The data was given in Parisian feet. The sea level of the bath site was fixed at 1,495 Parisian feet.

An attractive spa achieves perfection only in unity with the surrounding countryside. It is supposed to take effect in its entirety by combining healing and spa treatment with active recreation in a charming environment with correspondingly favorable climatic conditions. The importance of this factor for a stay in a health resort is documented by the fact that every spa patient spends an average of 5 hours outside every day regardless of the season. They walk approximately 12 kilometers (7.5 miles) and during a 25 day stay at the health resort cover the respectable distance of almost 300 kilometers (186 miles). This presents an indispensable and also calculable measure of the effect of the therapy on top of the actual treatment.

Examinations by health resort doctors prove that due to these activities the circulation becomes more stable and the heart activity more economical. With the covering of many kilometers, a high systolic blood pressure decreases more considerably than in other cases. Also metabolic processes take a more favorable turn with such patients, which can be seen from the development of the body weight.

Invigorating walks can without difficulty be taken in the outer area of the health resort. For this purpose a system of paths has been constructed for all levels of strain. The starting point of all paths was established at the edge of the inner spa area. Since walks on these paths are only taken during the therapy-free time, their length was limited corresponding to the local conditions. On hiking paths people walk from one place to the next, whereas here they always return to the health resort. Therefore, they are called terrain spa paths and are also differentiated with respect to their steepness so that the patients can choose a certain level of exertion and avoid excessive strain.

All paths radiate out to a ring-shaped path which at the same time forms the end of the respective paths and thus the destination. The paths were established in such a way that the hiker encounters an inn at this destination where he can rest. In order to return to the health resort can take a different path. He can use the ring-shaped path to get to the adjoining spa path and return on it to the health resort. Those who would like to become familiar with the valley basin of Bad Elster and get an overview of the area should use the terrain spa path since the ring-shaped path which is 18 kilometers (11.2 miles) long takes at some point the character of an elevated path and offers from

Ansicht von Alt-Adorf, 1626.　　　　　　　　　　　　*View of Old Adorf, 1626.*

gleiche Weg gewählt zu werden. Auf dem Ringweg kann man zu einem angrenzenden Kurweg gehen und diesen als Rückweg nach dem Kurort nutzen. Wer den Talkessel von Bad Elster richtig kennenlernen und überschauen will, der sollte die Terrainkurwege erwandern, denn der 18 km lange Ringweg verläuft an einzelnen Stellen als Höhenweg und bietet von verschiedenen Seiten Blick auf das im Kessel liegende Bad Elster. Die Möglichkeiten zur Gestaltung von Spaziergängen sind dabei so vielfältig, daß sie kaum während eines Kuraufenthaltes voll ausgeschöpft werden können.

Wer gut zu Fuß ist, der sollte auch größere Wanderungen nicht scheuen. Das obere Vogtland ist eine interessante Landschaft, die eine Reihe von Sehenswürdigkeiten bietet, die auch von Bad Elster aus auf größeren Spaziergängen zu erreichen sind.

Lohnend ist ein Besuch des *Musikinstrumentenmuseums* in Markneukirchen, das nach einer eindrucksvollen Wanderung über die Remtengrüner Höhe erreicht wird. Aus dem Fundus eines früheren Gewerbemuseums hat sich hier eine der bedeutendsten Musikinstrumentensammlungen Europas entwickelt. Sie ist im sogenannten Paulus-Schlössel untergebracht und wurde erst 1987/88 inhaltlich und thematisch völlig neu gestaltet. Im Hauptgebäude befinden sich Exponate vogtländischer Herkunft. Als ältester Zweig steht dabei der Geigenbau im Mittelpunkt, der Markneukirchen in aller Welt bekannt und berühmt gemacht hat. In einer Geigenbauerwerkstatt wird dem Besucher Einblick in die Lebensweise der Musikinstrumentenbauer um die Jahrhundertwende vermittelt. Umfangreiche Exponate von Musikinstrumenten aus aller Welt ergänzen die wertvollen Sammlungen.

Unweit davon entfernt liegt das *Bauernmuseum Landwüst.* Der Weg beginnt in Bad Elster auf dem «Almweg», weiter über Reuth-Sohl, vorbei am Raunerhammer und hinauf nach Landwüst. Weithin sichtbar grüßt von der höchsten Stelle (640 m) die kleine Dorfkirche. Über diese Höhe führte einst eine wichtige Straße hinüber nach Böhmen.

In einem der schönsten Egerländer-Fachwerkgiebel-Häuser aus dem Jahre 1782 wurde das Bauernmuseum eingerichtet. Die Ausstellungsstücke, vor allem viele tägliche Gebrauchsgegenstände, wurden von dem Bauern Walter Wunderlich gesammelt und zusammengetragen. Besonders wertvoll ist die Ausstellung von alten landwirtschaftlichen Geräten zur Bodenbearbeitung und zur Feldbestellung. Nach dem Besuch des Museums sollte man nicht versäumen, dem 664 m hohen Wirtsberg mit seiner Schutzhütte einen Besuch abzustatten. Ein herrlicher Rundblick bietet sich bis hinunter in das untere Vogt-

various sides an interested view of Bad Elster which is located in the basin. The possible variations of hikes are so manifold that they can hardly be exhausted during one stay at the health resort.

Good hikers should not shy away from longer walks. The Upper Vogtland is an interesting countryside which offers a number of sites which can also be reached during longer walks starting at Bad Elster.

A visit to the *Museum for Musical Instruments* in Markneukirchen is also worthwhile and can be reached after an impressive hike via the Remtengruener elevation. From the equipment of a former handicraft museum, one of the most important collections of musical instruments in Europe has developed. It is accommodated in the so-called Paulus castle and was completely redesigned with respect to contents and themes only in 1987–88. In the main building there are exhibits from the Vogtland. As the oldest branch, violin building which made Markneukirchen world famous is in the center. In the shop of a violin maker the visitor is given an idea of the way of life of the builders of musical instruments at the turn of the century. Comprehensive exhibits of musical instruments from all over the world supplement the precious collections.

In its proximity is the *Landwuest Farm Museum.* The path begins in Bad Elster at the «Almweg» (meadow path) and leads via Reuth-Sohl and Raunerhammer to Landwuest. From its highest point (640 meters [2,100 feet] above sea level) the small village church welcomes the visitor. An important road used to lead over this elevation to Bohemia.

The farm museum is accommodated in one of the most beautiful Egerland half-timbered houses with bay window from 1782. The exhibits, primarily many objects of daily use, were collected and gathered by the farmer Walter Wunderlich. Particularly precious is the exhibition of old agricultural appliances for cultivation of soil and fields. After a visit to the museum the 664 meter (2,180 foot) high Wirtsberg Mountain with its refuge should not be missed. From its top the spectator enjoys a marvelous view down to the lower Vogtland.

Those who would like to become really familiar with the countryside of the Upper Vogtland should take a hike to *Bad Brambach* on an elevated path. Via the Kellergrundweg path the hiker climbs up to the elevation of the Plattenberg Mountain and further to the Guerther cross where he traverses the road Raun-Guerth. Here is the stump of a mighty birch, a famous natural monument which was destroyed during a hurricane-force storm in November of 1984. From the opposite valley flank of the Raunerbach Brook one can see from the elevation Landwuest and its church at the upper edge of the village.

land. Wer sich einmal richtig mit der obervogtländischen Landschaft vertraut machen will, sollte eine Wanderung nach *Bad Brambach* auf dem Höhenweg unternehmen. Über den Kellergrundweg steigt man hinauf zur Höhe des Plattenberges und weiter zum Gürther Kreuz, wo die Straße Raun – Gürth überquert wird. Hier steht noch der Stumpf einer mächtigen Birke, ein bekanntes Naturdenkmal, das durch einen orkanartigen Sturm im November 1984 vernichtet wurde. Von der gegenüberliegenden Talflanke des Raunerbaches sieht man von der höhe Dandwüst mit seiner Kirche am oberen Dorfrand. Kurz vor Brambach wird die Wasserscheide erreicht. Bis zu dieser Schwelle fließt das Wasser über den Raunerbach zur Weißen Elster nach Norden. Danach aber ändert sich die Fließrichtung, nämlich zunächst im Röthenbach-Fleißenbachtal in südöstlicher Richtung und weiter zum Egerfluß. Im Röthenbachtal befindet sich das Zentrum des Heilbades Bad Brambach mit seinen Quellen und Sanatorien. Im Süden liegt das Gebiet des westböhmischen Bäderdreiecks, das über die Grenzübergangsstellen Schönberg bzw. Vojtanov (Voitersreuth) leicht erreicht werden kann. Nur Stichworte sollen genannt sein: Františkovy Lázne (Franzensbad) (6 km von Vojtanov, Kurort mit einer Parkfläche von 228 ha. Lohnender Ausflug zum Hochmoor Soos sowie zum Kammerbühl); Karlovy Vary (Karlsbad) (57 km von Vojtanov, ein Weltkurort mit über 600jähriger Tradition, Goethe-Gedenkstätten, heiße Sprudelquellen); Mariánské Lázne (Marienbad) (41 km von Vojtanov, weltbekanntes Heilbad mit großer Tradition, wertvolle Sprudelquellen, zahlreiche Parkanlagen in einer günstigen landschaftlichen Lage am Rande des Kaiserwaldes).

Zur Kur nach Bad Elster

Seit Jahrhunderten haben die Heilbäder und Kurorte zur Heilung und verbesserter Leistungsfähigkeit vieler Kurpatienten beigetragen. Die Wertschätzung der Kurortbehandlung war jedoch in den vergangenen Kulturepochen starken Schwankungen unterworfen. Schon von den Griechen und Römern wurden Bäder in Verbindung mit Gymnastik zur Erhaltung, Stärkung und Herstellung der Gesundheit empfohlen. Im Mittelalter finden sich zahlreiche Schriften, die empirisch auf die nützliche Wirkung von Bädern hinweisen. Die Badeeinrichtungen des Mittelalters waren jedoch vorwiegend Stätten des Lebensgenusses. Man traf sich mit Freunden zum Baden, zum Trinken und Schmausen. Die zweisitzigen Wannen wurden nicht selten von Personen verschiedenen Geschlechts benutzt. Die über viele Stunden ausgedehnten Badezeiten wurden durch Musizieren und allerlei gesellige Abwechslung im Bade kurzweiliger gemacht. Ein grundlegender Wandel des Kurwesens vollzog sich im 17. Jahrhundert. Die Bäder wurden zu Stätten vornehmer Gesellschaft, und die Trinkkur sowie die «Brunnenpromenade» lösten weitgehend die alte Bäderbehandlung ab. Im 19. Jahrhundert blühten zahlreiche Badeorte und Wasserheilanstalten auf. In der zweiten Hälfte des vergangenen Jahrhunderts begann man die Balneotherapie auf wissenschaftliche Grundlagen zu stellen.

Durch geologische Besonderheiten und Auswirkungen junger vulkanischer Tätigkeit entstanden im obervogtländischen Gebiet zahlreiche Mineralquellen mit reichem Kohlensäuregehalt, so auch in Bad Elster, Bad Brambach, Sohl und in den benachbarten böhmischen Orten der CSFR.

Der Plauener Stadtphysicus G. Leisner veröffentlichte im Jahre 1669 seine umfassenden Erkenntnisse über den Säuerling beim Dorfe Elster und seine Anwendung zur Heilung der verschiedensten Erkrankungen. Er betonte in der über 213 Seiten umfassenden Schrift: »Ich pflege aber Gläser zu brauchen/weil in solchen die liebliche helle und durchsichtige crystallinische Schönheit des Brunnens/so das Glaß gleichsam mit Perlen behefftet/denen Augen fürstellig gemacht,

Shortly before Brambach the watershed is reached. Up to this threshold, the water flows via the Raunerbach Brook to the Weisse Elster River to the north. Then, however, the direction of flow changes, at first in the Roethenbach-Fleissenbach valley to a southerly direction and further to the Eger River. In the Roethenbach valley is the center of the health resort Bad Brambach with its springs and sanatoria.

To the south the area of the West Bohemian bath triangle is located which can easily be reached via the border crossings at Schoenberg and Vojtanov. Only catchwords shall be mentioned: Franzensbad, 6 kilometers (3.7 miles) from Vojtanov. Health spa with a park area of 228 hectares (563 acres). Worthwhile excursion to the high swamp Soos as well as to Kammerbuehl. Karlsbad, 57 kilometers (35 miles) from Vojtanov. A world famous health resort with 600 years of tradition, Goethe memorials, hot springs. Marienbad, 41 kilometers (25 miles) from Vojtanov, a world famous health resort with a long tradition, precious springs, numerous park facilities, in a favorable location at the edge of the Kaiserwald forest.

For Health Treatment to Bad Elster

For centuries healing baths and health resorts have contributed to curing many health resort patients and to improving their efficiency. The appreciation of health resort treatments has, however, been subject to strong fluctuations in past cultural epochs. Already the old Greeks and Romans recommended baths combined with gymnastics for the preservation, strengthening and maintenance of health. In the Middle Ages numerous writings point out the empirically proven useful effect of baths. The bath facilities of the Middle Ages, however, were primarily sites for the enjoyment of life. Here people met with their friends for bathing, drinking and eating. The bathtubs with their two seats were more often than not used by persons of the opposite sex. The bath times which extended over several hours were made less boring by musical entertainment and all sorts of social distractions at the bath site. A basic change in the concept of health resorts took place in the 17th century. The baths become sites of noble society and the drinking cure as well as the «fountain promenade» largely replaced the old application of baths. In the 19th century numerous bath sites and water healing resorts came into bloom. In the second half of the last century balneo-therapy was placed on a scientific basis.

Due to geological peculiarities and effects of recent volcanic activities, numerous mineral springs rich in carbonic acid came into being in the area of the Upper Vogtland, for example in Bad Elster, Bad Brambach, Sohl and in the adjoining Bohemian towns of Czechoslovakia.

The Plauen town physician G. Leisner published in 1669 his comprehensive insights about the mineral spring at the Elster village and its application for healing various diseases. In his writings which comprise more than 213 pages, he emphasized the following: «I am accustomed to using drinking glasses because in them the agreeable light and transparent crystalline beauty of the fountain arouses in the patient a strange appetite and desire to drink, since the glass seems to be covered with pearls and introduces the mineral water to the eyes.»

Renowned scientists and medical doctors of Saxony, especially

und hierdurch denen Patienten eine sonderbare appetitus und Lust zum trincken erweckt wird.»

Namhafte Wissenschaftler und Ärzte Sachsens, so insbesondere Prof. W. A. Lampadius, Chemiker in Freiberg, Prof. J. L. Choulant, Geh. Medizinalrat in Dresden, und Prof. J. A. Stoeckhardt, Chemiker in Chemnitz und Tharandt, untersuchten im engen Kontakt mit Sachsens wissenschaftlichem Zentrum in Dresden seit etwa 1800 die im Dorfe Elster zu Tage tretenden Mineralquellen, deren besondere Wirkung und auffallender Geschmack bei den dort Wohnenden immer bekannter wurde. Die ersten Kurgäste kamen, und unter einfachen Verhältnissen wurden Trink- und Badekuren genommen.

In Erkenntnis, welche Möglichkeiten sich durch die Nutzung der Quellen für die meist armen Bewohner von Adorf und Elster bieten könnten, setzte sich der unermüdlich tätige Bürgermeister K. G. Todt zusätzlich für die «Emporbringung» der Elsteraner Quellen ein. Der Jurist Todt war in den 30er und 40er Jahren eine sehr einflußreiche Persönlichkeit, nicht nur im oberen Vogtland. Seine Beziehungen reichten bis nach Dresden als Abgeordneter, Regierungsrat und späteres Mitglied der Provisorischen Regierung des Revolutionsjahres 1849. Im Jahr 1835 ergriff er mit namhaften Persönlichkeiten anderer vogtländischer Städte die Initiative, ein «Comité zur Emporbringung des Elsterbades» bzw. außerdem die «Elsterbrunnen-Akziengesellschaft» zu gründen. Todt war es auch, der 1846 der Königlich-Sächsischen Regierung empfahl, den noch nicht 30jährigen Arzt Dr. Robert Flechsig (1817–1892) als Brunnenarzt am Elsterbad anzustellen. Am 1. Juni 1847 übernahm er sein Amt in Elster. Mit großem Engagement nahm sich der junge, aufgeschlossene Arzt der Mineralquellen des Elsterbades an, untersuchte sie wiederholt gründlich und arbeitete an ihrer Sicherung. Der Aktienverein bestand bis 1848/49; dann wurde das Bad von der Sächsischen Regierung unter der Regentschaft von König Friedrich August II. übernommen.

Trinkhalle der Königs-, Marien- und Albertquelle am Badeplatz 1875, heute Marienquelle.

Drinking hall of the Koenigs, Marien and Albert springs at the bath site, in 1875. Today, Marien Spring.

Professor W.A. Lampadius, chemist in Freiberg, Professor J. L. Choulant, medical counselor in Dresden, Professor J. A. Stoeckhardt, chemist in Chemnitz and Tharandt examined in close cooperation with the scientific center of Saxony in Dresden since 1800 the mineral springs surfacing at the Elster village near the town of Adorf, the special effect and striking taste of which became increasingly known to the inhabitants. The first health resort patients arrived and drinking and bathing treatments were applied under simple conditions.

Realizing the possibilities of exploiting the springs for the mostly poor inhabitants of Adorf and Elster, the mayor K.G. Todt, who was already untiringly working for the well-being of Adorf, also promoted the Elster springs. The lawyer Todt was a very influential personality in the 30's and 40's of the last century, not only in the Upper Vogtland. His connections reached to Dresden as representative, government counselor and later member of the provisional government of the revolutionary year 1849. In 1835 he, together with well-known personalities of other towns in the Vogtland, initiated the foundation of a «committee for the promotion of the Elster bath» and furthermore of an «Elster spring corporation». It was also Todt who in 1846 recommended to the Royal Saxon government to employ the medical doctor Robert Flechsig, who was not yet 30 years old, as spring physician at the Elster bath. On June 1, 1847 he took office in Elster. With great commitment the young, open-minded physician dedicated himself to the mineral springs of the Elster bath, repeatedly examined them thoroughly and helped to secure them. The corporation existed until 1848-49; then the bath was taken over by the Saxonian government under the rule of King Friedrich August II.

The first official bathing season at the Elster bath was in 1848 when 129 guests were counted. In that year which was so important for Bad Elster already four mineral springs existed. Further springs were discovered during regulatory work at the Elster River. Their securing from a viewpoint of building technology was realized systematically even though it was not highly welcomed by most Elster inhabitants at the time.

There was local peat in the area of today's gondola pond up to the region of the later sports stadium. After the peat had been exploited, the quantity necessary for the provision of the patients was gained at other high swamps of the Vogtland.

Bad Elster as Royal Saxonian State Bath started competing with the West Bohemian baths Franzensbad, Marienbad and Karlsbad. The number of health resort guests from Germany and from countries near and far (USA, Russia) continually increased. The necessary building facilities such as bath house, spring buildings, pump hall and so forth were repeatedly adjusted to the requirements. Stagnations and set-backs in Bad Elster were due to the First World War, the period of inflation and the Second World War. In the past few decades the possibilities for the expansion of buildings were rather limited, although efforts were made to modernize the «Bath of the Working Class» and to increase the number of cures spread out over the entire year as «scheduled». Unfortunately a decay of the building substance of many buildings took place, especially of bed and breakfast places the majority of which date back to the 19th century. This development can today only be reversed at great expense.

In 1966 the two state baths Bad Brambach and Bad Elster were combined. In the second half of the 1980's approximately 34,000 patients came to both health resorts every year and were taken care of by more than 1,300 employees of the state health care system.

But let us again return to the turn of the century. In 1903 Dr. Paul Koehler came to Bad Elster. The personality of this physician who was appointed honorary citizen in 1939 is connected with Bad Elster by three landmarks of his work:
– foundation of a sanatorium for physical healing methods (especially x-ray therapy of diseases);

Die erste offizielle Badesaison am Elsterbad war im Jahre 1848 mit 129 Kurgästen. Es gab in jenem für Bad Elster so bedeutungsvollen Jahr schon vier Mineralquellen. Weitere Quellen wurden bei Flußregulierungen der Elster entdeckt. Ihre bautechnische Sicherung wurde systematisch verwirklicht, auch wenn es von den meisten damaligen Elsteranern nicht freudig begrüßt wurde.

Eigene Moor(Torf)-Vorkommen gab es im Bereich des heutigen Gondelteiches bis hin in das Gelände des späteren Sportstadions. Nach dem Versiegen der Moorvorkommen wurde die zur Versorgung der Patienten notwendige Menge aus anderen Hochmooren des Vogtlandes gewonnen. Bad Elster als Königlich Sächsisches Staatsbad trat die Konkurrenz zu den westböhmischen Bädern Franzensbad, Marienbad und Karlsbad an. Die Zahl der Kurgäste aus Deutschland und dem nahen und fernen Ausland (USA, Rußland) nahm ständig zu. Die erforderlichen baulichen Einrichtungen, wie Badehaus, Quellenhäuser, Wandelhalle usw., wurden immer wieder den Erfordernissen angepaßt. Stagnationen und Rückschläge brachten der Erste Weltkrieg, die Inflationszeit und der Zweite Weltkrieg auch für Bad Elster. In den letzten vergangenen Jahrzehnten waren die Möglichkeiten zur baulichen Erweiterung sehr eingeengt, obwohl viele Anstrengungen unternommen wurden, das «Bad der Werktätigen» zu modernisieren und die Zahl der Kuren ganzjährig verteilt «planmäßig» immer weiter zu erhöhen. Leider kam es zu einem jetzt nur unter hohem Kostenaufwand wiedergutzumachenden Verfall der Bausubstanz vieler Gebäude, insbesondere der Pensionshäuser, die zu einem hohen Anteil noch aus dem 19. Jahrhundert stammen.

1966 wurden die beiden Staatsbäder Bad Brambach und Bad Elster zusammengeschlossen. In der zweiten Hälfte der zurückliegenden 80er Jahre kamen etwa 34 000 Patienten jährlich in beide Badeorte, versorgt von über 1300 Mitarbeitern des staatlichen Gesundheitswesens.

Kehren wir aber nochmals zur Jahrhundertwende zurück. – Im Jahre 1903 kam Dr. Paul Köhler (1864–1940) nach Bad Elster. Die Persönlichkeit des 1939 zum Ehrenbürger ernannten Arztes verbindet sich mit Bad Elster durch drei Marksteine seines Schaffens:
– Gründung eines Sanatoriums für physikalische Heilmethoden (besonders Röntgen-Therapie von Erkrankungen)
– Errichtung der Sonnenlichtheilstätte «Heimdall» für Kinder mit speziellen schwer heilbaren Formen der Tuberkulose und orthopädischen Leiden.
– Gründung eines Rheuma-Forschungsinstitutes mit Rheuma-Heilanstalt. Diese wissenschaftliche Einrichtung wurde seit 1945 schrittweise auf die Fachgebiete Kurort-, Krankenhaus-, Wasser- und Umwelt-Hygiene profiliert und als «Forschungsinstitut für Hygiene und Mikrobiologie» 1987 zu einem Kooperationszentrum der Weltgesundheitsorganisation ernannt. Anfang 1991 wurde dort eine Forschungsstelle des Bundesgesundheitsamtes eingerichtet. Aus dem einstigen Köhlerschen-Rheuma-Forschungsinstitut ging außerdem 1957 das heutige Forschungsinstitut für Balneologie und Kurortwissenschaft hervor. Sein langjähriger verdienter Leiter war Prof. Dr. Herbert Jordan (1919–1991), Ehrenbürger 1991 von Bad Elster.

Die Kurortbehandlung macht sich folgende Wirkprinzipien zu eigen: die Ausschaltung schädlicher Einflüsse, die Übung körpereigener Regulationen, die Steigerung der Organkapazität durch Anpassungsleistungen und die Gesundheitserziehung.

In ihrer gesellschaftlichen und medizinischen Funktion stehen die Heilbäder und Kurorte heute jedem sowohl bei gefährdeter Gesundheit, im Krankheitsfall oder zur Rehabilitation zur Verfügung. Kurkliniken und Sanatorien prägen das Bild vieler Heilbäder und haben weitgehend die Dominanz der Grand- und Palast-Hotels der Vergangenheit abgelöst. In Bad Elster gibt es heute drei Trinkquellen (Marienquelle I und III, Moritzquelle) und weitere fünf Quellen, die zu Badezwecken verwendet werden.

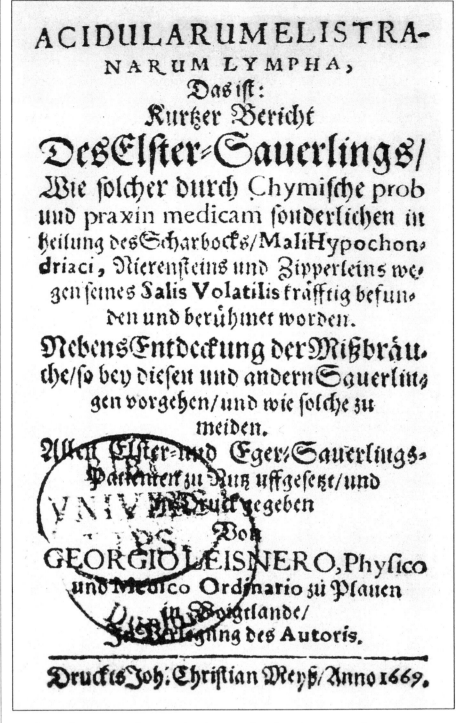

Titelblatt des 1669 in Plauen gedruckten Buches des Plauener Stadtarztes Georg Leisner (1609–1684).

Title page of the book by the Plauen town physician Georg Leisner (1609–1684), printed in Plauen in 1669.

– establishment of the healing facility «Heimdall» based on sunlight therapy, for children with forms of tuberculosis which were particularly difficult to heal and with orthopaedic ailments;
– foundation of a research institute for rheumatism with a healing facility for rheumatism. This scientific facility has since 1945 slowly profiled itself in the areas of hygiene for health resorts, hospitals, waters and the environment and has been named as «Research Institute for Hygiene and Microbiology» as a cooperation center for the World Health Organization in 1987. At the beginning of 1991 a research department of the federal health office was established there. The former Koehler Institute for Rheumatism Research was in 1957 turned into today's Research Institute for Balneology and Health Resort Science. For many years its merited head was Prof. Dr. Herbert Jordan (1919-1991), honorary citizen of Bad Elster.

The health resort treatment appropriated the following principles: the exclusion of harmful influences, the exercise of the regulatory system of the body, the increase of organ capacity by adjustment and health training.

Nach den seit den Anfängen bis zur Gegenwart ausgeführten chemischen Quellenanalysen handelt es sich in Bad Elster um Natrium-Sulfat-Chlorid-Hydrogenkarbonat-Säuerlinge. Die Elsteraner Trinkquellen eignen sich besonders zu Trinkkuren bei chronischen Magenerkrankungen und bestimmten Nierensteinleiden. Die Trinkkuren müssen individuell abgestimmt werden und bedürfen einer ärztlichen Überwachung. Neben diesen Trinkquellen erforderte der ständig anwachsende Badebetrieb von Jahr zu Jahr mehr Quellwasser. Die Bade- und Balneotherapie mit Mineral- oder Kohlensäure-Bädern wird vorwiegend zur Behandlung von Herz-Kreislauf-Erkrankungen, wie z. B. Bluthochdruck, Mangeldurchblutungen des Herzens, Zustand nach Herzinfarkten und funktionellen Herzerkrankungen angewandt.

Die unspezifischen Effekte der Bäder beruhen auf mechanischen Einflüssen und auf thermischen Komponenten. Spezifische Wirkungen werden überwiegend durch die im Bad vorhandenen Inhaltsstoffe, von denen das Kohlendioxid eine wichtige Rolle spielt, ausgelöst. Bad Elster ist eines der ältesten Moorbäder und genoß einst den Ruf, Deutschlands größtes Moorbad zu sein. Die balneotherapeutische Nutzung des Moores im Thermotherapieverfahren geschieht auf Grund seiner hervorragenden physikalischen und chemischen Eigenschaften. Die wichtigsten Inhaltsstoffe sind Humusstoffe, Gerbstoffe, östrogene Substanzen, Spurenstoffe usw.

Das Moor wird in den verschiedenen Applikationsformen vorwiegend bei Erkrankungen des rheumatischen Formenkreises sowie bei dermatologischen und gynäkologischen Erkrankungen therapeutisch genutzt. Auch das Heilklima des Kurortes – als ein Bestandteil natürlicher Heilmittel – spielt eine wichtige Rolle. Bedingt durch die Tallage Bad Elsters und die umliegenden Berge kommt es zu Temperaturschwankungen im Tagesverlauf; diese Rhythmik wirkt sich für den Klimadesadaptierten günstig aus. Weitere Vorteile des Elsteraner Kessels bestehen in der Schutzwirkung gegenüber dem wechselhaften Witterungsablauf unserer mitteleuropäische Breiten und in der vielfältigen landschaftlichen Aufgliederung, durch die es zu unterschiedlichen Besonnungsverhältnissen kommt. Das natürliche Heilmittel «Klima» wird ebenfalls u. a. durch die Einrichtung eines Terrainkurwegnetzes, das zu einer gezielten aktiven Bewegungstherapie anregen soll, für den Kurpatienten genutzt.

Der Kurpatient, der nach Bad Elster kommt, kann diese natürlichen Heilmittel im Rahmen einer «Kurorttherapie» nutzen. Unter diesem Fachbegriff versteht man die Komplexität aller in einem Kurort zur Anwendung kommenden Heilmethoden, die zwar vorrangig die naturgegebenen Heilmittel, aber ebenso die Methoden der Physiotherapie und die erforderlichen pharmakologischen und psychotherapeutischen Behandlungen einschließt. Ihr besonderes Charakteristikum liegt in der kurmäßigen Applikation ihres Ablaufes und der reaktiven Leistung des behandelten Organismus. Kurverfahren werden als Kuren im stationären Bereich in modernen Rehabilitationseinrichtungen oder als offene Badekuren in privaten Pensionen durchgeführt.

Seit Anfang 1991 werden in enger Zusammenarbeit zwischen Stadtverwaltung, Landratsamt und Regierung des Freistaates Sachsen spürbare Veränderungen in der Struktur des Badeortes unterstützt und gefördert. Neue Klinikbetriebe werden in vorhandener Bausubstanz eingerichtet, wie Hurrle-Klinik, Vogtlandklinik und Paracelsusklinik. Neubauten und bauliche Erweiterungen werden folgen.

Bad Elster als Kurort und Heilbad hat alle Chancen – eingebettet in eine wunderschöne obervogtländische Landschaft, aufgrund 150jähriger Tradition als Heilbad, den Besitz natürlicher Heilmittel und eines erfahrenen medizinischen Behandlungspersonals sowie in einer sich ständig verbessernden Infrastruktur – sich erneut zu einem Kurort von internationaler Bedeutung zu entwickeln.

In their social and medical function the healing baths and health resorts are today available to everyone in the event of endangered health, in case of disease or for rehabilitation purposes. Health resort clinics and sanatoria characterize the picture of many spas and have largely replaced the domineering grand and palace hotels of the past. In Bad Elster there are three drinking springs today (Marien springs I and III, Moritz spring) and another five springs which are used for bathing purposes.

According to the chemical spring analyses which have been performed from the beginning to the present day, Bad Elster provides the minerals natrium, sulfate, chloride, and hydrogen carbonate. The Elster drinking springs are particularly suitable for drinking cures in case of chronic stomach diseases and certain kidney stone problems. The drinking treatments must be adjusted to the individual and be applied under medical supervision. Apart from these drinking springs, the continuously increasing bath operation requires every year more spring water. The bathing and balneological therapy with mineral and carbonic acid baths serves primarily for the treatment of heart-circulatory diseases like for example high blood pressure, lack of blood circulation in the heart, the state after cardiac infarct and functional heart diseases.

The unspecific effects of baths are based on mechanical influences and thermic components. Specific effects are primarily triggered by the contents of the bath, among which carbon dioxide plays an important role.

Bad Elster is one of the oldest mud bath resorts and once enjoyed the reputation of being Germany's largest mud bath resort. The balneo-therapeutical exploitation of the mud in thermic therapy is based on its eminent physical and chemical features. The most important ingredients are humus, tanning agents, estrogenic substances, trace elements, etc.

Physicians use the mud in its various forms of application primarily with rheumatic diseases as well as dermatological and gynecological ailments as therapy.

Also the healing climate of the health resort – as part of natural means of healing – plays an important role. Due to the valley location of Bad Elster and the surrounding mountains, there are temperature changes in the course of the day; this rhythm has a favorable effect on people disadapted to climate. Further advantages of the Elster basin lie in its protective effect against the changeable course of weather of our Middle European climate and in the varied countryside which results in different sun conditions. The natural means of healing «climate» is also used, among other things, through the establishment of a terrain health spa path network which is intended to inspire a directed active movement therapy for the health resort patient.

The health resort patient who comes to Bad Elster can use these natural means of healing within a framework of a «health resort therapy». Its special feature lies in its application within a health resort program and the reaction of the treated organism. Spa therapy is carried out as cures in the stationary area in modern rehabilitation facilities or as open bath cures in private bed and breakfast places.

Since the beginning of 1991 considerable changes in the structure of the bath site have been supported and promoted in close cooperation between town administration, district office and government of the Free State of Saxony. New clinics are included in the existing building substance such as the Hurrle Clinic, the Vogtland Clinic and the Paracelsus Clinic. New buildings and expansions will follow.

Bad Elster as health resort and healing spa has every chance – embedded in the beautiful landscape of Upper Vogtland, its 150 years of tradition as health resort, its possession of natural means of healing and an experienced medical therapy staff as well as in continually improving infrastructure – to again develop into a spa of international importance.

Die Farbtafeln

33 Blick von der Mittagsseite auf den Kirchberg.

34 Badehaus, Alberthalle, 1909 von den Architekten Schilling und Graebener erbaut.

35 Wandelhalle, vom Fuße des Brunnenberges aus gesehen. Errichtet von den Architekten Kramer und Dutzmann 1928/29 im Bauhausstil.
Als Baumaterial diente Postelwitzer Elbsandstein. Brunnenschale von Bildhauer Hempel, Dresden, 1966.

36 Badehaus, Alberthalle. Ausstattung durch Bildhauer Gross, Dresden, 1909.

37 Badehaus, Kuppelhalle im Waldflügel, erbaut 1882/83 vom Landbaumeister Waldow. Das Deckengemälde und die Reliefs erinnern in ihrem Stil an die Semperoper Dresden.

38 Badeplatz, die von Hermann Schüttauf 1933/34 gestaltete Anlage. Im Hintergrund das alte Badehaus von 1851/52.

39 Gondelteich, auf dem Gelände eines Moorstiches 1893-1904 von Paul Schindel als «Louisa-See» angelegt.

40 Marienquelle, die neue Quellenhalle entstand 1933/34 bei der Umgestaltung des Badeplatzes durch die Architekten Kramer und Dutzmann. Die Quelle selbst wurde um 1800 entdeckt und gefaßt.

41 Marienquelle und Brunnenschale. 1956 von Fritz Kühn geschaffen.

42 Hygiea, Denkmal im Albert-Park hinter dem Kurhaus, von Bildhauer Hultsch, Dresden, 1887. Ursprünglicher Standort an der alten Wandelbahn zwischen Moritz- und Salzquelle.

43 Kurhaus mit Parkanlage, 1888–1890 erbaut.

44 In der Trinkhalle der Moritzquelle. Älteste, seit Jahrhunderten bekannte Mineralquelle Bad Elsters.

45 Die Elster an einem Tor zum Hof des Badehauses.

46/47 Kurzentrum, Luftbildaufnahme mit Blick zum Brunnenberg.

48 Rathaus. 1916 errichtet als Gemeindeamt, erweitert 1935/36.

49 Evangelisch-Lutherische Kirche «St. Trinitatis», 1889 bis 1892 nach Plänen des Architekten Christian Schramm, Dresden, im neugotischen Stil errichtet.

50 «St. Trinitatiskirche», unter der Südempore.

51 «St. Trinitatiskirche», Chrorraum mit den beiden aus dem 15. Jahrhundert stammenden Apostelfiguren Petrus und Paulus.

52 «Palasthotel Wettiner Hof», nach einem Brand von den Architekten Zapp & Basarke, Chemnitz, errichteter Jugendstilbau. Seit Anfang der 80er Jahre nicht mehr als Sanatorium genutzt. Die Sanierung wurde begonnen.

53 Römisch-Katholische Kirche, «St. Elisabeth», 1913 geweiht.

54 Stadion im Elstertal. Blick von der Römisch-Katholischen Kirche «St. Elisabeth» auf die 1931 unter Leitung von Gustav Allinger errichtete Anlage.

55 Haus «Hygiea», Pension in der Parkstraße. Erbaut um 1880.

56 Haus «Pax». Kurpension in der Parkstraße. Errichtet 1899.

57 Kurtheater. Errichtet von den Architekten Zapp & Basarke, Chemnitz, als Nachfolgebau des alten «Cursalons». Eröffnet 1914 durch König Friedrich August III. von Sachsen.

58 Klinikum «Sachsenhof» an der Badstraße. Erbaut 1914 an Stelle des «Hotel de Sax» von den Architekten Zapp & Basarke, Chemnitz

59 Kurhotel «Haus am See». Fertiggestellt 1989 am Standort des ältesten Elsteraner Gasthofes, der seit 1848 den Namen «Reichsverweser» trug.

60 Rehabilitationsklinik «Albert Funk», Endersstraße.

61 Vogtland-Klinik. Fertiggestellt 1982.

62 Haus «Betula», Pension in der Prof.-Paul-Köhler-Straße. Erbaut um 1900.

63 Haus «Linde». Kurheim in der Beuthstraße. 1807 als Gerichtshaus errichtet. 1892/93 Umbau im Neorenaissancestil.

64 «Heimdall». Rehabilitationsklinik für Kinder und Jugendliche, Haus «Sonnenhöhe».

65 Hotel «Central» in der Johann-Christoph-Hilf-Straße.

66 Haus «Marienbrunnen». Pension in der Badstraße. Errichtet um 1860.

67 Im Rosengarten. Teil des Parkes, der seit 1883 auf dem Areal des ehemaligen Rittergutes angelegt wurde.

68 Weiße Elster. Blick von der Dammwegpromenade.

69 Kreuzkapelle am Brunnenberg. Errichtet 1877. Im Sommer finden in dieser Kapelle Waldgottesdienste statt.

70 Blick vom Brunnenberg in Richtung Ortsteil «Kessel».

71 «Holländerei». Aussichtsterrasse am Brunnenberg.

72 Halbmeilensäule der «Cursächsischen Post». Errichtet 1724 durch Adam Friedrich Zürner an der alten Poststraße Adorf-Elster-Asch. Jetziger Standort: am Kirchplatz gegenüber dem Rathaus.

73 Adorf, «Freiberger Tor». Mittelalterliches Stadttor der alten Stadtbefestigung. Heute Museum der Stadt.

74 Adorf. Stadtrechte seit 1293. Rathaus, 1896 nach einem Brand neu erbaut.

75 Markneukirchen. Evangelisch-Lutherische Stadtkirche «St. Nicolai», spätklassizistischer Bau von 1848.

76 Markneukirchen, «Paulusschlössel». Spätbarocker Bau aus dem Jahre 1784. Beherbergt heute das 1883 gegründete Musikinstrumentenmuseum mit über 1000 Exponaten aus aller Welt.

77 Markneukirchen, Hausorgel im Musikinstrumentenmuseum. Gebaut von Orgelmacher Georg Hamer aus Schiers/Schweiz 1838.

78 Markneukirchen, Geigenmacherdenkmal vor dem Musikinstrumentenmuseum. Geschaffen von dem Bildhauer Franz Matuska.

79 Markneukirchen, Werkstatt eines Blechblasinstrumentenbauers.

80 Landwüst, Bauernmuseum. Butterformen auch «Modeln» genannt.

81 Landwüst, Bauernmuseum. Wohnstallhaus, 1782 erbaut.

82 Landwüst, Bauernmuseum. Stallboden mit Ausstellungsstücken.

83 Landwüst, Bauernmuseum. «Tripfhäusl», aus Tirpersdorf umgesetzt.

84 Landwüst, Dorfkirche «St. Laurentius». 1432 erstmals erwähnt, ausgestattet mit einer der wenigen erhaltenen Orgeln der Adorfer Orgelbauerfamilie Trampeli aus dem Jahre 1822.

85 Wirtsberg bei Landwüst (664 m), Schutzhütte auf der unbewaldeten Bergkuppe, errichtet 1985/86, Architekt Benno Kolbe.

86 Raun, Kapelle, neuerrichtet 1681 an der Stelle einer älteren Kapelle aus der Zeit vor der Reformation.

87 Wohlbach, Pfarrkirche «Zu unserer lieben Frau», Altarraum 1200 bis 1258 bereits als Marienkapelle geweiht.

88 Raun. Untere Mühle mit Egerländer Fachwerkgiebel, jetzt Reiterhof.

89 Gunzen. Griebenherd.

90 Schönberg, südlichster Ort Sachsens. Blick vom Kapellenberg (759 m) nach Böhmen.

91 Wirtsgrund bei Erlbach, Grenzstein der Sächsisch-Böhmischen Grenze aus dem Jahre 1544.

92 Klingenthal. Rundkirche «Zum Friedefürsten», erbaut 1736/37. Eine der wenigen erhaltenen Rundkirchen Sachsens.

93 Klingenthal. Blick vom Aschberg (936 m).

94 Oelsnitz/Vogtland. Rathaus, nach einem Stadtbrand in den Jahren 1861/62 errichtet.

95 Plauen. Altes und Neues Rathaus am Altmarkt. Renaissancegiebel mit Uhr aus dem Jahre 1548.

96 Schöneck. Blick ins Vogtland vom «Alten Söll» (734 m).

33 View from the midday side toward the Kirchberg Mountain.

34 Bath house, Albert Hall, built in 1909 by the architects Schilling and Graebener.

35 Pump house seen from the foot of the Brunnenberg Mountain. Established by the architects Kramer and Dutzmann in the Bauhaus style in 1928-29.

Elbe sandstone from Postelwitz was used as building material.

Fountain bowl by the sculptor Hempel, Dresden, 1966.

36 Bath house, Albert Hall. Designed by sculptor Gross, Dresden, 1909.

37 Bath house, domed hall in the forest wing built by the master builder Waldow in 1882–83. The painting on the ceiling and the reliefs are reminiscent of the Semper Opera in Dresden.

38 Bath site, the facility designed by Hermann Schuettauf in 1933–34. In the background, the old bath house from 1851-52.

39 Gondola pond which was built on the area of a peat cutting as «Louisa Lake» by Paul Schindel in 1893–1904.

40 Marien spring. The new fountain hall was erected during the reconstruction of the bath site by the architects Kramer and Dutzmann in 1933-34. The spring itself was discovered and lined around 1800.

41 Marien spring and fountain bowl. Created by Fritz Kuehn in 1956.

42 Hygiea monument in the Albert park behind the spa house, created by the sculptor Hultsch, Dresden, 1887.

43 Spa house with park facility, built 1888–90.

44 In the drinking hall of the Moritz spring. Oldest mineral spring of Bad Elster, known for centuries.

45 The Elster River at a gate to the courtyard of the bath house.

46-47 Spa center, aerial photograph with view toward the Brunnenberg mountain.

48 Town hall. Erected in 1916 as administrative office for the community, expanded 1935–36.

49 St. Trinitatis Lutheran Church built from 1889 to 1892 according to plans by the architect Christian Schramm, Dresden, in the neo-Gothic style.

50 St. Trinitatis Church, below the south choir.

51 St. Trinitatis Church, choir area with the apostle figures of Peter and Paul, both dating back to the 15th century.

52 Palace hotel Wettiner Hof, an art nouveau building constructed after a fire by the architects Zapp & Basarke, Chemnitz. It has not been used as a sanatorium since the beginning of the 80's. Renovation has begun.

53 St. Elisabeth Roman Catholic Church consecrated in 1913.

54 Stadium in the valley of the Elster RivView from the St. Elisabeth R.C. Church towards the facilities which were built in 1931 under the guidance of Gustav Allinger.

55 «Hygiea» house, bed and breakfast facility on Park Street. Built around 1880.

56 «Pax» house, spa bed and breakfast facility on Park Street. Built in 1899.

57 Spa theater. Built by the architects Zapp & Basarke, Chemnitz, to succeed the old «Cursalon» (spa salon). Opened in 1914 by King Friedrich August III of Saxony.

58 The «Sachsenhof» Hospital on Bad (bath) Street. Built in 1914 in place of the «Hotel de Sax» by the architects Zapp & Basarke, Chemnitz.

59 Spa hotel «Haus am See» (house on the lake). Completed in 1989 at the site of the oldest Elster inn, which since 1848 bore the name «Reichsverweser» (protector).

60 «Albert Funk» Rehabilitation Hospital on Enders Street.

61 Vogtland Hospital. Completed in 1982.

62 «Betula» House, bed and breakfast facility on Professor Paul Koehler Street. Built around 1900.

63 «Linde» House, spa accommodation on Beuth Street. Built in 1807 as court house. Redecorated in the neo-Renaissance style in 1892–93.

64 «Heimdall» Rehabilitation Hospital for children and youth, «Sonnenhoehe» (sunny height) House.

65 Central Hotel on Johann Christoph Hilf Street.

66 «Marienbrunnen» (Marien spring) House, bed and breakfast facility on Bad (bath) Street. Built around 1860.

67 In the Rose Garden, part of the park which was planted since 1883 on the area of the former Knight's Estate.

68 Weisse Elster River. View from the dam promenade.

69 Kreuzkapelle (cross chapel) on the Brunnenberg Mountain, erected in 1877. In summer forest services take place in this chapel.

70. View from the Brunnenberg Mountain to the village district of «Kessel».

71 «Hollaenderei». Panoramic terrace on the Brunnenberg Mountain.

72 Half-mile pillar of the Post of the Electorate of Saxony. Established in 1724 by Adam Friedrich Zuerner on the old Post road Adorf-Elster-Asch. Presently located on the church square opposite the town hall.

73 Adorf's «Freiberg Gate». Medieval town gate of the old fortification. Today, the town museum.

74 Adorf, a chartered town since 1293. Town hall, rebuilt after a fire in 1896.

75 Markneukirchen. St. Nikolai Lutheran Town Church, late Classicistic building from 1848.

76 Markneukirchen, «Paulusschloessel» (Paul's castle). Late Baroque building from 1784. Today it accommodates the museum of musical instruments which was founded in 1883 and houses more than 1,000 exhibits from all over the world.

77 Markneukirchen, home organ in the museum of musical instruments. Built by organ builder Georg Hamer from Schiers, Switzerland in 1838.

78 Markneukirchen, violin maker monument in front of the museum of musical instruments. Created by sculptor Franz Matuska.

79 Markneukirchen, workshop of a brass wind instrument builder.

80 Landwuest, farm museum. Butter molds.

81 Landwuest, farm museum. Living and stable house, built in 1782.

82 Landwuest, farm museum. Stable attic with exhibits.

83 Landwuest, farm museum. «Tripfhaeusl» house, moved from Tirpersdorf.

84 Landwuest, St. Lawrence village church. Mentioned for the first time in 1432, equipped with one of the few remaining organs of the Adorf organ builder family Trampeli from 1822.

85 Wirtsberg Mountain, close to Landwuest (664 meters [2,179 ft]). Refuge on the unforested mountaintop, built in 1985-86 by the architect Benno Kolbe.

86 Raun Chapel, newly built in 1681 at the site of an older chapel from the time before the Reformation.

87 Wohlbach, «Our Blessed Virgin» Parish Church, altar area consecrated already in 1200–1250 as Mary's Chapel.

88 Raun, lower mill with Egerland half-timbered bay window. Now a riding stable and inn.

89 Gunzen, «Griebenherd» stove made of stones in the form of a fountain for boiling pitch in order to shoe horses.

90 Schoenberg, southernmost spot in Saxony. View from the Kapellenberg Mountain (759 meters [2,490 ft]) to Bohemia.

91 Wirtsgrund close to Erlbach, border stone of the Saxonian-Bohemian border from 1544.

92 Klingenthal. «Zum Friedefuersten» (to the prince of peace) round church built in 1736-37. One of the few remaining round churches in Saxony.

93 Klingenthal. View from the Aschberg Mountain (936 meters [3,071 ft]).

94 Oelsnitz/Vogtland town hall, built after a town fire in 1861–62.

95 Plauen. Old and new town halls at the Altmarkt (old market). Renaissance gable with clock from 1548.

96 Schoeneck. View into the Vogtland from the «Alte Soell» (734 meters [2,408 ft]).

51

„Butterformen"

„Kässteig"

Denkmal

GRIEBENHERD/PECHPFANNE

Diente bis zum 19. Jahrhundert
zur Gewinnung von Pech aus
harzigem Holz, welches für
die Hufpflege und als
Wagenschmiere
Verwendung fand.

Rat der Gemeinde Gunzen